The Day They Took My Son

TEMIKA SMITH HARDEN &
MONTRAE KORNEGAY

CONTENTS

PREFACE

October 1, 2017

The worst day of my life…

The guys at the house jumped up from the table and quickly headed out the door. My sister Shan and I felt it in our spirit that something was wrong especially when she yelled out what is going on and did not receive a response. They continued to quickly walk out the door. I tried to call each one of the guys that left the house but none of them answered. After speaking to my stepdaughter Kiki who was so emotional yelling and crying. I finally got in contact with my cousin JJ, who was one of the guys that had left the house earlier. While speaking to him I heard two loud banging noises coming through the other end of the phone. At this point I did not know my life was about to change. Then I got a beep on the other end. When I answered I heard a familiar voice say "Meka, he been shot, and he is not responding". So many things began to go through my mind; I began to pray that everyone was okay. All the while, screaming and crying; hoping it was all a dream.

I sit back and think about everything that went on that day and try to make sense of it all. Why didn't I get up and follow Dre, JJ, Niq, Buck, Marco, and Rj when they left my house? Why didn't I make them answer my sister when she questioned them? I am striving every day to keep my son's memory alive, but my body seems to shake from the inside out every time I even think back to that night. I try to focus on all the good times I had with my him to ease the pain. However, I can't help reliving that tragic day over and over again. The First 48 did an episode about my son's case but I didn't like the story they told so here's my story.

C H A P T E R   1

The Birth of a King

Waking up the morning of Christmas 1997 I felt deep pains in my stomach. I still managed to get up and shower to get prepared to go to my sister's house for dinner. Although, I was in pain I was determined to eat Christmas dinner. My sister Bonnie had made collard greens, cornbread, dressing, chitterlings, candy yams, and potatoes salad. I was full and the pain started to get deeper; and I knew at that point it was time for me to dial 911. I was getting ready to have my baby boy, my Christmas baby. He was an addition to my already growing family. I decided to combine all our names to come up with a name for our new addition. My first-born King/son Dominique, my name Temika, and his father's name Chico. We welcomed Domiquo, (Meco) Riley on Christmas night 1997. There I was holding my Christmas baby; He was my second-born son. It's so strange to think back, it's like he was an angel from birth. One of my best friends would jokingly tell everyone his name was Jesus. He was a mama's boy, he always wanted to be with me. His dad would get upset and he would blame it on the fact that I breastfeed him.

When Meco was in Elementary school I never had any problems with him. Calls from school would be to ask "if everything was ok at home" because he was so quiet. A few different teachers over the years called or emailed to say how "they wished they had other children in the class as kind and polite as Domiquo was". He only spoke in class when the teachers called on him; he wouldn't ask for help. They knew how bashful he was so they would check on him periodically to make sure he was catching on to the work.

Domiquo began playing football, basketball, and softball at the age of four. He was good at all three sports, but football was his favorite. He was the quarterback on his team for several years. We would jokingly say he must do sign language to his teammates to tell them what plays to do because he would barely talk to any of them. When he did speak or say something it was so soft, they could barely hear him. But once he got in the game you forgot all about how quiet and laid back, he was. He left all of that on the sidelines and became a different person. He played hard and he truly came alive when playing any kind of sport.

When he started to grow up and become a teenager, he loved himself some soul food; chitterlings being his favorite (which was one of the things I had eaten right before bringing him into the world). It amazed us how he stayed so thin. He was also very clean cut. His clothes always had to be neat and ironed and he HAD to have a haircut. If his hair was not cut, he would ALWAYS wrap a bandanna around his head. It didn't matter what kind of bandana as long as it matched his outfit for the day. If he could not find a bandanna, he would take my winter scarves and wrap them around his head so that nobody could see that his hair was not cut to perfection. Meco was so full of style; he would wrap the headscarf in such a way that it looked nice with his outfits and stylish glasses. My other children, as well as the children in the neighborhood, started wrapping winter scarves around their head as a part of their outfit for the day.

When Meco got to his high school years I would talk to him about what his goals were once he graduated from high school. He told me he wanted to own an auto repair shop. I laughed so hard because Meco was my child that did not even like to get his hands dirty. He had long nails that always looked like they were freshly manicured. I said to him, "son how are you going to work at an auto repair shop when you don't like to get your nails dirty?" He said, "Ma you didn't hear me right I don't plan to work there I plan to own it". I always knew Meco would be a go-getter and a hard worker.

8

Soon after he graduated, he got a job at an auto parts warehouse. He started up a 401K plan and instantly began to save his money. He then purchased himself a 2008 model Chrysler 300. He would always call it "his little baby". He paid his own car note and I helped with half of his insurance. He was working so hard to make his way in this world, only to have his life taken from him less than a year later. He was only 19 years old.

C H A P T E R   2

Family Day

The morning of September 30, 2017 seemed to be just another regular morning, but little did I know the torment it would lead to. I opened my blinds looking out to see the sun shining bright. It looked as if the weather would be perfect to match my plans for the day. My sisters Shan and Bonnie were both coming into town and I was so excited. This didn't happen often or at the same time because one lives in Alabama while the other lives in Ohio. Today was a special day because my nephew Brandon had a modeling event in Atlanta. I was happy to be able to support my nephew. I reached out to all my children asking if they would like to attend the event. A few of the children could not attend. Domiquo was unsure while my stepdaughters Mercedes and Kiki said they would attend, along with 2 of Kiki's friends Nieya and Dionna. We usually do not use the word step in our house however, to give you a better understanding of his story, I decided to. Nieya had been Meco's girlfriend through most of his high school years and even though they had broken up she still came around the family often because she was close friends with Kiki.

When I went downstairs, the children that lived in the house were sitting in the living room talking, playing, and enjoying their time together. Domiquo was always quiet around people he did not know but when he was around family and friends his personality really shined. He would always give his sisters and brothers a hard time. He would wrestle and joke around with them but on this day, he hugged his little sister Mesha and told her he loved her. He also had a good conversation with his younger brother Marco (whom he bothered the most).

Although he was very open with the family at home, when it came to showing affection to his siblings, he was still kind of bashful. That is why these incidents stand out in my mind. My husband, Ade and I have a combined family of nine children. My husband has five: three girls and two boys and I have four: three boys and one girl. They always give each other a hard time; horse playing and wrestling around with one another. Some people have said they could not tell that we were not related by blood. They could not believe that my husband and I were not the biological parents to all the children. This was outside of his oldest daughter Marie because a lot of people did not know her. She is married, with two children and lives in Virginia.

As we got closer to the time of the event, my sister Shan arrive, we talked about how the children were growing up. She had expressed an uneasy feeling she had before she came to visit about 1 1/2 months prior. During that visit, she told me she wanted to get our sons together so she could pray over them and anoint them with holy oil. She expressed her frustration because she had left the oil at home this time.

Before going online to purchase our tickets for the show later that night I reached out to Domiquo. He was the only one that had expressed interest but had not given a definite answer. Him and his girlfriend, Nae was out having lunch when I called. He said they wanted to attend the show, so I proceeded to purchase their tickets as well. We arrived at the event where we met up with my sister Bonnie and her son Brandon; We exchanged hugs. I began to play with my little cousin Ricky (also known as Peeper's son). Seeing the baby caused me to get emotional because his father/my cousin had been killed that March due to gun violence. Trying to move past the sadness, I began to joke around, talk and laugh with my family members.

I had been watching the door to see if the rest of the family would arrive so I could wave them over to the area that we were sitting in. I was trying to save them a seat next to us, but the seats were filling up fast. I then see my nephew Buck, Mercedes, Kiki, Dionna, and Nieya with Meco and Nae right behind them. I noticed a young man stopped Meco and Nae just as they were walking in and started to talk to them. I thought that maybe there was a problem, so I started to get up. Just as I was about to get up from my seat, the man who had been speaking to them, picked up a camera and got into a position to take their picture. I had been watching the door for a while however I had not seen him stop anyone else to take a picture. This was the third weird thing that happened on that September 30th night. I remember feeling like things were awkward because Domiquo seemed reserved and quiet especially since he was around family. I asked him if he was okay. He said yes. I did not press the issue any further, thinking maybe he felt weird because his new girlfriend Nae was there as well as his ex-girlfriend Nieya.

When we arrived at my house my husband Ade, my youngest son Marco, and his friend RJ were already there. My sisters and I sat in the living room running our mouths and catching up since we hadn't seen each other in a while. By the time we got settled in and my sister's grandchildren in bed it was slightly after 12am the morning of October 1, 2017. This day would turn out to be the worst day of my life and it was less than two hours into the day.

Everything was going great and most importantly most of us were going to be together. All the young men were sitting at the dining room table playing cards, laughing and talking trash to one another. About 20 minutes goes by…my nephew Buck shows up but, neither Meco nor Mercedes were anywhere to be found. I asked him where they were because they rode to the event with him. He told me they'd decided to go to an open mic night performance of one of Mercedes' friends. It was located at a nightclub in Norcross, GA. I was kind of upset because I had expected everyone to come back to the house; it was a good opportunity for us to spend time together. However, I did not force the issue; I have spent several days beating myself up mentally about it. I still to this day wish I had.

CHAPTER 3

Why Didn't They Just Leave

While sitting in the living room talking to my sisters; suddenly all of the guys who were playing cards in the dining room stood up, grabbed their belongings, and left in a hurry. This caught our attention and my sister Shan yelled "what's going on, where's everyone going?!", "I don't know but something is going on"! I yelled "let's follow them!" said Shan. I was standing there in only a spaghetti-strapped nightshirt, matching bottoms and some house slippers. I yelled back "but we don't know where they're going". My motherly instinct kicked in and told me to call my two sons that still lived in the house but were not home yet. Neither one of my sons had been in any kind of trouble or any huge confrontations but I still went with my first instinct. I began quickly dailing Meco's number. When he answered the telephone a sense of relief went through my body. "Are you ok", I asked. "Yes", he said. He told me he was at a club called Midnight Blu in Norcross. They had just been put out because some guys, that had about twenty-five people with them, tried to make him take off the blue dress shirt he was wearing; but he refused to do so. Then some guys walked into his face and popped him on the nose with a bandana. Who's with you, I asked. He replies, OG, Mercedes, Nieya, Kiki, and Nae but I'm okay. We're leaving now and we are on our way to the house. "Ok, come home. You need to leave now!" I said. I knew that had to be where the guys in the family were headed. I tried to call my nephew Dre' to tell them to come back to the house but Dre' did not answer. Then I called my nephew Buck; however, he did not answer his phone either. Finally, I called my daughter Kiki and when she answered she was screaming and telling me to please make them get in the car so they could leave. "What is going on?" I asked. "They won't leave the parking lot of the club! They want to go in and talk to the guys that approached Meco", she yelled. I was nervous now so much, that I forgot to ask Rukiya where the club was. I told her to let me call them then I hung up. I called my cousin JJ and told him I needed him to get everyone in the car and leave. "Meka we are all getting in the cars to leave now" he said. Something in my spirit did not feel at ease so I asked again "is everybody in the car?". Before he could reply, I heard a loud "Pow-Pow" sound. I jumped up from the couch yelling through the phone, "Were those gunshots?!!!" My sisters yelled in unison, "What!" I began to yell through the phone, "Go!!!...Go!!!…" as my body began to tremble. JJ yelled back we're going Meka! Is everyone in the car, I asked while still yelling. Yes! he said.

In the pit of my stomach it felt like something was not right. My phone rang. It was my stepdaughter, Mercedes; she's crying and yelling, "He's been shot Meka and he is not responding!". Who? I asked. She said, "Meco!" Where are you all??? The phone went silent, she had hung up. I clicked back over to my cousin JJ. I was yelling, crying, praying, and running to the car at the same time. I had no idea where I was going. I was still on the phone with JJ telling him exactly what Mercedes had told me. At the same time, my husband Ade, Joi my oldest son's girlfriend and I were all enroute to the nightclub. This is the club where they had tickets to see someone perform.

My sisters started running out the door as well, but they soon remembered they're grandchildren, were still in the house. They were too young to be left alone so they had to turn around and stay at the house. Where are they, I yelled to JJ? I don't know Meka he yells back? I hung up on him, I tried to call Mercedes back but there was no answer. I tried calling Nae but no answer. I then tried to call Kiki but again, no answer. I began to panic even more. I needed to tell them what to do for him, how to help him. I still needed to do a mother's job even if it was from a distance and in a really bad situation. I then called my stepson, Lil Ade, to ask if he knew where they were? No, why what is going on? Ask, Lil Ade. Upset because no one seemed to know where Meco and Mercedes were…I lost it!

When my mind snapped back, I was upside down on the passenger side of my car, kicking and screaming. Ade was driving so fast he almost made us flip over into a ditch. I don't even remember my next set of thoughts, but the feeling of anxiousness began to make me feel like I could not breathe. I do not remember how we found out where they were. The next memory I have is of us pulling up on Jimmy Carter Blvd. There were police cars everywhere. They were lined so far down the street that we had to leave the car abandoned in the middle of the road. We jumped out the car down by the Chick-Fil-a restaurant that's located on the corner. We had to run to the Shell gas station. As I ran down the street the lights from all the police cars were so bright. Nieya was running towards me yelling, "No Mrs. Temika, tell him to come back" as she was jumping up and down crying. It felt like my legs were going to give out on me at that point, but I had to make it over to him. There might be something I could do. I had been praying on the way there and they say what you ask God for you shall receive. When I made it to the Shell gas station (after what seemed like forever), I see my nephew Buck struggling with the police officers. He's trying to get to my son who was lying on the ground with a sheet on top of him. God had failed me on the most important thing I had ever asked for in my life. Why would he do such a thing to me? I always help others. I take care of everyone else's children in the neighborhood. I could hear everyone around me screaming and crying but it seemed so distant and faint. It was as if everyone was on the 10th floor of a building and I was on the first floor all alone. People were walking up and hugging me but I'm not even sure who because it was as if I was having an out of body experience.

Still standing outside of the Shell gas station with my emotions all over the place; my cell phone rang. I had forgotten I was even holding it in my hand. It was my cousin Ev, who lives in Cincinnati, OH. She called to ask what was going on? She had heard Meco got shot. "He's gone Ev", I said. When they said Meco I told them they had to have it wrong, it had to be one of the other kids because no one would have a reason to bother Meco. I told her it was him, but I had to call her back because I was still at the scene (in a very monotone voice). The call with my cousin Ev made me realize I needed to call my mom; although I knew someone had probably already called her. I took a deep breath; I needed to try to calm down before I spoke to my mom who still lives in Cincinnati, OH. She is very close and protective of all her grandchildren. To hear her cry from so far away was going to hurt me to my heart. I knew she would be home alone but if she could just hear my voice. I could try to reassure her that I was feeling better than I was. After hanging up with my cousin Ev, I began to make the call that I dreaded to make.

My fingers trembled as I tried to pull up my mom's number in my phone. I thought I had it together but as soon as she picked up, I began to cry, and my cry became more and more uncontrollable. I felt as if I could not breathe again. My words were broken, and they were barely coming out of my mouth. All the while trying to tell her they had killed my baby. "Oh No!", she yelled. She began to cry while asking what happened. I couldn't get my words out so I mumbled and told her I would call her later.

I then had to call Chico, Meco's dad. Chico lives in Alabama; the children would visit him on holidays or during long weekend breaks from school. I knew this call would be just as hard as the call I had to make to my mom. When he answered the phone, I immediately said, "Chico, they killed Meco" barely getting the words out. "What!!! What the f !", said Chico. Then there was complete silence. After a short while he asked, "what happened?" I told him I would tell him later. He was on his way back home from out of town and he was not driving so he asked me to keep him posted on what was going on. I was too consumed with sadness to be angry at him. It frustrated me not to hear him say he would be on his way to Georgia as soon as possible. But now was not the time to worry about it.

Just as I was starting to calm down some a detective walked over to me and asked if I was Mom. I faintly said yes. The first thing she said to me sounded muffled but whatever she said made my husband upset. So much so; he began to yell something back to her in a very loud voice. My mind was in such a fog that his words were not coherent to me. Her response to him was, "we are going to find out who did this and if you have any questions call me." Then she handed me her business card. The only thing that stuck out to me was when she said, "we are going to find out who did this".

Once she said this; the fact that I was standing at a crime scene; a crime scene where my 19-year-old son, Domiquo (Meco) Riley, laid on the ground lifeless, came back to me. JJ, my cousin, was right by my side hugging me and trying to comfort me. However, I could see the hurt all over his face as well. I then noticed how many people were there in the gas station parking lot and I realized my sisters had made it there. I look over and I see my stepson, OG, with his face all bruised up. I immediately went to his aid. I ask him if he was ok or if he needed to go to the hospital? I'm ok, he said. I tried to convince him to go to the hospital to get checked out, but he refused. He still seemed to be shaken up, so I did not ask him any questions about what transpired. I then notice that Nieya and Kiki were sitting in the back of the police car for questioning. Nae, Meco's girlfriend, was on the ground screaming and crying with her mother standing over her trying to comfort her. However, I did not see my stepdaughter, Mercedes anywhere. I began to question what happened and where she was. Someone yelled out that she had gotten into a car and left. I did not understand how she could leave my child lying on the ground dead.

My sister-in-law Niecy walked up to me. She said, Mercedes called her and told her what had happened. She then goes on to say, "it would have been nice if Mercedes would have stayed to tell me what happened. I told her to call you". I have not seen her out here at all. Where is she, I asked. "Due to another situation she had going on she got scared and left," said Niecy. I was furious. There was no reason good enough for her to leave Meco's side while he was dying. A thousand things went through my mind and none of them were good. Someone is going to tell me what happened to my son, I said to no one in particular.

CHAPTER 4

He Say, She Say, Begins

A young lady, who I was not familiar with, came up to me. "Ms. I was there. I know of some of the guys involved. I tried to do CPR on Domiquo, but the police wouldn't let me. They pulled me away", she said while standing there looking very upset, shaken, and confused. I then asked her name and who were the people involved? It was a group of boys that call themselves Bloods. She went on to say that they were trying to start a fight with all the guys that came into the club. She said, security was only putting out the other people not them. She also said a girl with white hair gathered up the bloods to tell them that Meco and some others were standing outside. She didn't know any of the individuals' names, but I thanked her for the information she had given me. Once Meco's girlfriend, Nae, calmed down I began to question her about what happened. She said her and Meco had gotten in the car with Mercedes (who's, car was parked at the front of the club) so she could drop them off at Meco's car (which was parked further in the back of the club's parking lot).OG had gone back to the door of the club to wait for the club promoter, Terry. Terry had been cutting all our boy's hair since they were young. OG was waiting on Terry to give him back the $20 they had paid to get in the club because they had only been there for 15-20 minutes before they were kicked out. As they were driving to Meco's car they heard loud yelling. When they looked back there was a large group of people running out the front door of the club and they were fighting. They noticed that OG was in the center of the large group of people and he was trying to fight his way out. There were way too many people hitting him at one time. Someone in the car yelled "That's OG!!". Nieya, who was driving Mercedes' truck, pressed on the brake. Meco yelled "hell naw" and jumped across me, Mercedes, and Kiki laps to try to help him. He had only run a short distance from the truck when we heard gunshots. Meco turned around and started running back to the car as gunshots continued to ring in the air.

When he reached the car, he slumped over across our laps face down. I yelled "Meco!!!" but there was no response. Then I felt a warm liquid running down my legs. Calling his name again I looked at my hands to see what it was, and I realized it was blood. "Oh no he's been shot; he needs to go to the hospital" I yelled. Nieya began to drive and bullets began hitting the truck. While trying to dodge the bullets and get Meco legs in the truck; we lost track of where OG was. We rode around the parking lot a few times before we found him laid out on the ground. KD, Mercedes boyfriend helped put OG in the hatch back of the truck. There was not any time to put his legs completely inside because bullets were flying everywhere. We pulled out of the club parking lot into a closed Chevron gas station and quickly put OG legs inside. As we were pulling out of Chevron Kiki dialed 911. In the meanwhile we decided to go towards the hospital ourselves. We headed to highway 85 North when Mercedes told Nieya to pull into the Shell gas station because there was not enough gas in her truck to make it to the hospital. At the time you could hear the sirens from the ambulance flying past on the other side of the median. We stopped and pulled Meco from the car and laid him on the ground. Kiki was yelling on the phone to the 911 operator, asking where they were going because they did not make the U-turn to come back to us; they kept going in the direction of the club. Kiki ran inside the gas station to get the address to give to 911. A girl ran over and started trying to perform CPR on him by this time the police pulled up and began to push us back. They did not even try to perform CPR on him Nae said. My legs felt weak. I did not want to hear any more right now it was too much for me. It was too much for Nae too as she tried to continue her story, but she began panting and breaking down again. We would have to finish some other time. I was so out of it I had not even noticed how cold it was; someone had taken their jacket and thrown it over my shoulders.

It was now 5 a.m. and we had been standing at the gas station since 2 a.m. I stood there watching as my son's body lay on the ground with a white sheet covering him. I still remember standing there as a gust of wind came through and blew the sheet off his face. "Cover my baby up!" I yelled. My nephew, Buck, instantly started to break through all the police officers that were standing there so he could replace the sheet over Meco's face. While the officers were trying to stop him from reaching Meco, he was also yelling at them to cover Meco.

When the police officers went over to Meco's body they blocked off the area with one of the police vans so we could not see when they lifted him and put him in the adjacent van. I knew it was time for them to take him away from me, but I was not ready. I was weak, angry, and all I wanted was to take my son home with me. "Don't take my baby!", I yelled. "Don't take my baby!" Several people rushed over and began to hug me; they tried to comfort me. But I did not feel any comfort at all, I felt empty inside like my body was there without my soul. Why couldn't they have taken me? My son had so much of his life ahead of him. There's nothing in this world that I wanted more than to watch my children become successful adults and great parents. My husband grabbed a hold of me and led me to the car.

CHAPTER 5

Trying to Make Sense of It All

I do not remember the ride home, nor did I notice that everyone in the family was following behind us. Once we arrived at my house, my cousin JJ, my nephews Dre and Buck, as well as my sons Niq and Marco, and their friend RJ sat in front of the house. My sister Shan and Bonnie were still crying with a look of disbelief on their faces. They did not say much they just grabbed their grandchildren and went inside. Ade was very upset; he was not in the mood to talk or be around others, so he went into the house. I could not bring myself to go into the house that I shared with Meco. It no longer felt like home; now it only felt like the house that he would never come back to. When I got tired of standing, I sat inside of my cousin JJ's truck. I just sat there and listened to the guys talk for hours. It was now daylight outside, and I was still sitting in the truck. I still could not walk into that house.

Sleep had not come over me nor had it crossed my mind. The guys got in and out of the truck while still talking about what happened as I continued to ask question after question. It seems as they were having a hard time wrapping their head around things and this was more than frustrating to me. None of them seemed to see what happened. Each of them tried to tell me their version of what occurred; however, none of them fully made sense. All I knew was I wanted my son and he was not coming home. I rolled up the window to the truck I didn't want to hear anymore. I needed to be alone. I was ready to leave so that I could find and kill the people responsible for murdering my son.

I needed to clear my head, so I texted my friend Nikki to see if she was awake. She quickly texted back yes, so I called her immediately. "They killed my baby!" I said when she answered the phone. Nikki was taken aback…What!! she yelled. Nikki… "they killed my baby", I repeated. In a much calmer tone. Oh no! Which one, she asked. She had so many questions. I had spoken to Meco about 30 or 40 minutes before the incident happened, I told Nikki. Then I began to tell her the story as it was first told to me. I started telling her how Meco sent a text message in the group chat that the guys from our old neighborhood as well as our family members were in. They used the group chat daily just to see what was going on for the day. When they received the text, they headed to the club he was at in Norcross because he told them what Kyese, the guy who had popped him in the face with the bandanna, and his friends had done to him. I told her how they had beat, my stepson OG then killed my son Meco. As I said this I again began to cry uncontrollably. Girl let me throw on some clothes; I am coming over, she said.

When I hung up with Nikki, I managed to get out of the truck to converse with my family members that were still standing on the porch. I was trying to take in any information that would help me pinpoint the person who killed my son. By the time Nikki arrived; I found myself sitting on the couch in a daze. I do not recall walking into the house or anything after that. She'd brought food with her, but I could not force myself to eat anything, but I thanked her for the gesture. Have you been to sleep at all asked Nikki? I told her I could not sleep, and that sleep was the furthest thing from my mind. When I was asked this question, it prompted me to look at the clock and I realized it was 10 am. My phone had been on vibrate and I had several missed calls. My family members and friends in Cincinnati had been calling as well as my friends and family in Georgia and Alabama. I did not have it in me to return any calls yet.

Again, I asked the guys in the family who were at the house how Meco had gotten shot; Each of them said they did not see Meco out in the parking lot, so they did not know how he ended up getting shot. We were all in the cars trailing each other to leave that's why we cannot make sense of how this happened, said JJ. I will get to the bottom of it if my life depends on it, I said. The news played about the incident repeatedly on every local channel. They described the scene as looking like the "Wild Wild West" because there were over 100 shell casings found. The windows were shot out of the cars in the parking lot as well as the windows to the other businesses in the plaza. The news report said, "Meco had been shot twice in the chest" this was the first time I had heard he had been shot twice.

What a way to find out the details of my son's death. Was this even true? When the news aired again, I found out the police were looking for the security guard Christopher Parker for Meco's murder. They announced that he was hired as an armed security guard for the club despite previously doing thirteen years in jail for rape; as well as some other charges. I had not heard back from the detective yet and I was hoping it was because she was busy trying to find out who was responsible for my son's death. While sitting on the couch in a daze without one minute of sleep, and nothing to eat or drink; I thought over and over again about what I could have done to prevent this from happening. The phone rang again like it had been doing all day. It was my friend Heather; she asked if I needed her to bring my mom to Georgia. I was so grateful for a friend like her. I really needed my mom to be here with the rest of us. Although, we were all walking around the house looking like zombies (none of us could get any sleep); I did not want her to be alone.

Several of my family members went to sit with her for a few hours, but I knew they would only be able to come and go. For the next few hours, we all sat in the living room with blank looks on our faces. My husband stayed by my side tightly holding on to me. Some of those that were there dozed on and off; but not me. Someone offered food and water, but the thought made me sick to my stomach. My phone rang constantly so I spoke to several people who sent their condolences. I checked with Heather to see how my mom was holding up on the ride. "She is doing okay; I just keep talking to her to try to keep her mind off things. We are about to pull up shortly" she said. I thanked her again and hung up. An hour later

Heather and my mom pulled up to my house. Everyone went to the front of the house, watching as my mom got out of the car. As she got out; she immediately began to yell and cry. It was like a song of pain and hurt as all of us followed suit. We all gathered around her; hugging her and one another. Once we made it back into the house, she had us gather around and hold hands as she began to pray. There were sobs, sniffing, and screaming. You could hear the trembling in my mom's voice as she yelled for God to help us through such a tragic moment, for him to give us peace, and to wrap his loving arms around us. I was angry towards the God that she was calling out to. How can he help us now when he was the one that allowed this to happen? I did not need his help, Meco did... I thought back on the several mornings I knelt on the side of my tub to thank God for all the blessings in my life. I thought about how I prayed for him to protect my loved ones from any hurt, harm, death, or danger; seen or unforeseen. The bible says, "you ask, and you shall receive". Well I did not receive what I asked for and I was pissed. I do not remember much more about this night besides us all sitting around talking.

I still had not been to sleep and still could not manage to go upstairs to my bedroom. I remember it being around 3 a.m. before everyone began to settle down. I remember this only because someone mentioned the time. It was only a few hours from me being awake for 48 hours and sleep still had not crossed my mind. I felt like my eyes could not close even if I wanted them to. Sitting up on the couch for the second night watching my family members doze on and off. I watched the sunrise for the second day. I thought a lot about why I was still able to walk this earth. Meco had not been allowed to live his life yet. There were so many things for him to do. He had not been able to have a child to carry on his name. I was hurting so bad that I wanted to die. Once again, I began to cry uncontrollably until I had a headache. My family was finally able to convince me to take something so that I could sleep.

CHAPTER 6

Their True Agenda

My mom, friend and sisters had gone back home to get things situated so they could come back for the funeral.

I hated they had to leave because I was not sure what I would do or how I would handle what was being forced on me as my new normal. Sitting around thinking would not be good for me right now so I had to do something to occupy my time. I informed my job of what was going on and took a leave of absence. Although I needed something to do to keep busy, I knew I would not be able to focus on work. I had just gone back to school again one month prior but that was not something I could focus on either. So, I had taken a leave from school as well. I was cleaning my house which is something I have always did when I was upset. It always helped when I needed to redirect my energy in a positive direction. And today, I really needed to redirect my energy so I would not completely lose it. I was trying to keep the little bit of sanity I still had left.

While trying to clear my mind from everything that was going on; I received a call from Detective Kulnis of the Gwinnett County Police department. The detective reintroduced herself and I questioned the information the news had stated about Meco being shot twice. Detective Kulnis verified that Domiquo had been shot twice, once in the hand, and once in the back. Both bullets went straight through him but the one from his back traveled upward hitting his heart causing his death. I was then reassured that "she would get to the bottom of it". She then asked me if I could come to the station so she could speak to me as well as my relatives that were in the club parking lot the night Meco was killed.

We rode to the precinct in different cars; Buck and Dre in one car, Niq, Marco and I in another. When we arrived at the police station, they took each of us into separate rooms; I was put in the waiting room. The precinct was quiet and cold. It was around 8:30 pm so all the employees were already gone for the day except for the detectives that were there to speak to us. Detective Kulnis told me again that Meco had been shot in the hand and in the back; the bullet traveled upward and punctured his heart. It made me feel as if Meco saw his shooter aiming at him, he put up his hand to block the shot, then was shot a second time as he turned and tried to run away. The thought of my baby possibly seeing a bullet coming towards him made me upset. The thoughts I was having made the wait seem like forever. Sitting and thinking were not good for me. Tears began to roll down my face as I (again) thought about what I could have done to stop Meco, my second born son, from being murdered. How could I get revenge on the people involved? They should be sitting here... not Buck, Marco, Niq, Dre and me. Where were they? Had any of them been interviewed? Where was the guy who owned the barbershop? You know...the guy that was promoting what turned out to be a blood gang party at the club. Why wasn't he there being interviewed?

A man startled me as he walked into the room and sat on the chair in front of me. He was a Caucasian man of medium height and build. He was probably in his mid to late 30's. I quickly wiped my tears thinking he was another detective. This detective could not see me crying because he needed to know I meant business. He needed to know that I was serious. He needed to know that I was hurt, angry, in disbelief and that I would not let up for even a second until they found the ones responsible for Meco's death. The man leaned in towards me and extended his hand. He introduced himself as a producer of the TV show "The First 48". I Exhaled...I was just so happy and relieved to have someone to talk to. It would help to take my mind off everything that was going on. I was starting to get a headache. He introduced himself but my mind was in a fog so I cannot remember his name. He began to explain how the TV show "The First 48" had been following the detective that was working Domiquo' s (Meco) case. He went on to explain how long he had been working with the show and how they were at the scene the night Domiquo was killed. He then asked if I would allow them to do an episode on Meco's case. I told him I would get back to him. I had to think about it. He went on to say how "Domiquo was the first victim that he's seen in which no one has had one bad thing to say about them". I was happy to hear this but not very surprised because Domiquo was never a problem. Before the producer left out of the waiting room; he handed me his card and thanked me for my time. I continued sitting in the waiting room alone for about another thirty minutes while the detective questioned my family members. I thought about how "The First 48" could be a way to help catch the individuals responsible for Meco's death. I was not sure how my husband or his dad would feel about putting family business out in the public (even though it was not in a negative light). I wondered if Meco would approve of me allowing them to tell his story.

While in deep thought I heard a door open and then talking. The voice was familiar, it was the detective and she was speaking to my youngest son, Marco. The detective asked me to come into the room with her and Marco, she was convinced that Marco knew more than he was telling her, so she wanted me to have a talk with him to see if he would tell me anything. Confused about why Marco would withhold any evidence that would help the police put away the people responsible for killing his brother made me upset and sad. Trying not to come across as angry I explained to him what the detective said to me, I told him how bad it would hurt me if he knew something and did not speak up. "Ma, if I would have seen something, I would have already told you and you know that" said Marco. He then went on to say how he felt like they were trying to force him into saying something that he did not know. I assured him that he could tell me anything that came to his mind about the incident, no matter how small or irrelevant he thought it was. We sat in silence and I tried to fight back the tears that were building up. I knew Marco was trying to be strong for me, but I could tell he was hurting as well. When the detective came back, she asked if there was anything Marco wanted to talk to her about and I told her what he told me. "He did not see Meco as they were pulling out the parking lot or anyone else. He only saw my nephew, Buck and his friend RJ; whom he had rode to the club with.

CHAPTER 7

The Ride Home

O nce we left the precinct and went back to my house, we called Buck and Dre on my car speakers to talk about their interviews with the detectives. I came to find out everyone was very upset. They all regretted going to the precinct. They all said the detectives kept asking questions about who they were with. They asked several questions about people that consider themselves to be in a group called MBK. A group of children that moved to Georgia with no family became very close and hung together daily is what MBK is. It was not a gang, there was no leader, no specific color you could or could not wear, and most of the parents of the children knew one another. The name MBK came along when some of the young men decided to start rapping together so they needed a name for their group. The name extended to the entire group because of the things they did for one another. If one of them did not have anything to eat or nowhere to stay one of the other ones would take them in and feed them. They've done things like this for one another even if it meant they had to sneak to do it. The letters simply stand for My Brothers' Keeper. They were confused and continued to question why the detectives seemed to be more focused on individuals from the group, some who were not even out there the night Meco was killed. One of the questions I had asked myself while sitting in the waiting room was one of their questions as well. "Had the detectives questioned everyone that was at the scene of the crime, the people at the club that was clearly in a gang". "They are not worried about who killed Meco they're trying to find out about some gang stuff that Meco has nothing to do with", shouted Niq angrily. Feeling angry and now frustrated; I still tried to reassure my boys that, even though it did not seem like it, the police were doing what needed to be done to catch the people responsible. After dropping Niq off at home, Marco and I were in the car alone. Marco was one of the family members on the porch talking about what happened on the day of the incident. Things were a blur and I was still feeling like the story was scattered. I needed to hear from Marco about what he did know so, I blatantly asked him. He began to tell me they received a message in their group chat from Meco which is why they left the house when they did. Him, Buck, and Rj arrived at the club in one car, followed by JJ, Niq, and Dre in another.

When they pulled into the parking lot of the club Meco was standing outside with Nae, Mercedes, OG, Kiki and Nieya. They were standing near Mercedes' truck which was parked near the front of the club. When they walked up Meco was laughing as he began to tell them about the guys approaching him in the club. Meco expressed how he was upset that Kyese had popped the bandanna causing it to hit him in the face. However, Marco said Meco was giggling the whole time he is telling the story. He then told me, Dre and Mercedes were arguing about them going in the club and that Meco wanted to go back in too. When you called JJ and told him we needed to leave he summoned for everyone to get in the car to leave. Their car was the last car to pull out; at least that is what he thought. That's OG!!! RJ yelled. This caused Buck to immediately stop the car to see what was going on. About fifteen guys fighting OG, so they jumped out of the car and ran back towards the front of the club to help him. They then see OG being hit over the head with a Hennessy Cognac bottle. They run up and start fighting with some of the guys that were attacking OG and that is when the gunshots began to ring out. They ran back to the car and pulled away from the club. "That's why I do not understand how Meco got shot because I did not see him when they were running to help OG. I thought they pulled out the parking lot already" Marco said. My thoughts were all over the place while he was telling me the story. Why were they still out there? Where were Nae, Mercedes, Kiki, and Nieya? The car was quiet the rest of the way home as more and more questions began to pop into my head. I will not stop until I know every detail.

CHAPTER 8

Getting Prepared

Chico, the kids' father, came to town on Wednesday. He arrived from Alabama along with his father, Bell, Sholeka, his ex-wife, and his sisters Sylvia and Mika. My sister Shan, my mom, and my friend Heather were at my house as well. It was time to do something I never thought I would have to do; prepare to bury my son. There was so much that needed to be done but all I wanted to do was lie on the couch and stare at the wall. I am not sure what it was, but I still had not been able to sleep in my bed. My husband and I would push the couches together so we could sleep in the living room. Chico had a sad look in his eyes as he tightly hugged my weak body. Meco was the younger version of his dad. I caught myself staring at him wondering if Meco would have continued to look like him had he been given the chance to grow older.

I began to tell Chico about the different funeral halls I had researched and how I wanted to lay my son to rest nicely. "Temika, I can't do it, I can't go to help pick out no casket for him", he said. For a second, I wondered why he came if it was not to help, but I quickly changed my thoughts. I understood that he just wasn't strong enough to do it. Why did I have to be the strong one? I did not want to be the strong one in this situation. I did not feel strong. I wanted it all too just disappear. I wanted it all too just go away as if it never happened; but my motherly duties for Meco had to continue and unfortunately this was the only thing I could do for him.

My husband, Ade, said he would go but I wanted Chico and his family to be a part of Meco's home going as well. Since no other men were going to the funeral home; I suggested Chico's sisters and ex-wife come along to help make decisions on Chico's behalf. My husband could stay at the house to entertain Chico and his dad. I did not feel up to driving but I did because we all could not fit in one car. Shan and Heather were in one car and the rest of us in another. I remembered this funeral hall because my stepchildren's mother's funeral was held there a couple of years earlier.

When summoned to the room in the back by the owner of the Funeral home, Shan and Heather came along but Chico's sisters and ex-wife stayed up front, I was bothered. "Why did they come if they were going to distance themselves and not even going to listen or see what the funeral home had to offer"? When I thought about how I had driven in my state of mind, I became more upset. It was important to me that they be a part of this process however, I could not force it on them.

I quickly snapped back from the negative thoughts. I realized they may not have felt comfortable voicing their opinion about something that carried so much pain and emotion. I was drained and my drive to look for a funeral home was gone. Shortly after we got back to the house Chico came to me with a bothered look on his face. "They are ready to go", he said. "I know we have not been here long but I rode with them so I am on their time, I will be back and next time with someone who will not be in a rush to get back". Chico went on to tell me that October 1st, which is the day that Meco died, was his younger brother's birthday. His brother, Rico, died in a car accident at the age of 13. This happened a few years before I met Chico but every time, we talked about it I could still sense the pain he felt. It was like it just happened. Again, I was disappointed, but I understood his situation. Didn't they care about his other children? They needed him to be there for them as much as he could? Shouldn't this time be more about him? It had not even begun to get dark outside and they were ready to go. I could not allow it to bother me. There were too many other things that I had to worry about.

The next morning my husband and I went to visit several funeral homes. My sister, Shirley, stepped in to help; she was a blessing. She connected us to people that did Meco's makeup, the embalming, and they dressed him. I really hated to have her do this because she had just played a big part in the funeral arrangements of our sister, Diane, her twin, who had died on New Year's Eve 2016. She had also planned the funeral of their mom who died less than 2 months after Diane. My sisters Shirley, Diane, and Jackie are my sisters from my dad's side, as well as my sister Cynthia and my brother Lucius.

We visited a funeral home in Decatur, Ga, which was about 25 minutes from my house. It was nice, and I felt at ease when speaking to the young lady who worked there. We decided on a casket and an urn. We made the decision to have him cremated so we could always have him with us. My friend, Nikki, spoke with my job and they agreed to pay for the floral arrangements for the top of Meco's casket. I just needed to have them delivered to the funeral home. I wanted to make the obituary and the montage, I knew it would be hard, but I wanted it to be special. I had to have a hand in it to make sure it was right. It was also a way for me to continue to be Meco's mom. This was going to be one of the last things I could directly do for him. I can't remember a lot of the details from that day my mind often wandered, and I would periodically break down into tears. I constantly had to look through pictures to put in the obituary, the montage, and the book. My heart was broken; the empty feeling on the inside made me sick to my stomach. Everything had to be perfect, so I had to keep pushing.

People brought flowers, money, food and cards to the house daily and on most days a couple times a day. I still could not eat but I was very thankful because I did not have it in me to make sure my family ate. My sons' wrestling coach, Coach Hardy, was like an angel on earth. He spoke to the school for us to make sure the children's situation at the school was taken care of. He also came to the house every day with food, drinks, and offering whatever he could to help. We had people at the house all day every day paying their respects and showing support. My friends from the job were wonderful; they took turns coming to the house in groups to keep me company. They pitched in to make sure my family ate as well. Having such a great support system was a great help. I could not have imagined doing it without friends and family. I know I would have given up and died from a broken heart. People being there, showing love did not mend my heart nor did it lessen the sadness I felt; but it was a constant reminder. It was a reminder that I had something to live for along with the love for my other children, my husband, and my other loved ones.

CHAPTER 9

The Homegoing

My King's funeral was set for October 7, 2017. I decided to put him to rest dressed in white and sky blue. I dressed him in these colors because I knew he was going to the heavens above where the clouds were white, and the sky was blue. I gave my family and friends the information about the funeral arrangements. It was to be held at A. S. Turner Funeral home at 2 pm on a Saturday afternoon. I was praying that my son was in peace; I asked God if his death was an act of his, hoping I would hear an answer that would make me feel better.

Later that day, Meco began to show his presence. Several of us were sitting in the house talking and the doorbell rang. I cannot recall which of the children it was but one of them went to the door but when they opened it, no one was there. When they walked back into the house, they asked everyone else if they'd heard the doorbell ring and almost in unison everyone said yes. "No one was there" they said. Shortly after the doorbell rang again but again no one was there. Our front door has a keypad and a code to be entered to unlock the door. We could hear the buttons being pushed as if someone was trying to enter the code. Then we heard a long beep which is what would happen if someone entered the wrong code. When we would go to the door, no one would be there. This made me sad because I felt like Meco was trying to come home. He was stuck in the realm of life and death which to me meant he was not at rest. I wished that

I would open the door and he would be standing there even if not in the flesh in the spirit. My heart ached from the thought and it saddened me even more.

My loved ones really showed up for us; between my friends and family members, 35 to 40 traveled from near and far. Some came to town on Thursday evening and the rest on Friday; They came from Alabama, Cincinnati, and the Carolinas. I was so glad to see everyone here to send Meco off to be with our savior. It was the first time that several of them had been to our home. I was also glad that so many people were here for me in my time of need...I needed them like never before. My children's friend's moms came over to pay their respects. Each one, of them talked about how quiet, sweet, and respectable Meco was. Everyone; friends and family members alike, were all saying how they could not believe that something like this could happen to Meco.

The day before the funeral, my husband Ade, Meco's father Chico, my sister Shirley, my cousin Nika, and I went to view Meco's body. We wanted to make sure he looked perfect for his home going. It was so hard to see my son lying in the casket. I burst into tears and my knees felt wobbly. I did not want to leave him there. We all stood there silently for a moment before we left. I knew the next day would be the last time I would be able to touch my son and I was not ready. The wake started 2 hours before the funeral. When we arrived, the room was so full they had to clear a walkway for the immediate family to walk through. My heart felt empty... I'd lost weight from not eating but I'd barely noticed. There was nothing I could do for my 19 years old son who was lying in the casket in front of me. I sat down to give others a chance to pay their respects.

Suddenly I heard a loud painful cry a cry that sounded as if it came from the pit of a person's stomach. Then the word "why" followed in a loud screeching tone. I didn't have to look up I knew who it was; I knew the voice. It was my sister Bonnie. We were all in so much pain. A few months prior, we'd experienced the death of my first cousin, Ricky (aka Peeper) due to senseless gun violence in Ohio. His nickname was Peeper and he was like a son to my sister;

she helped raise him. The death of Meco was like cutting open a wound with nothing to numb it before it had a chance to heal.

When we went into the chapel, there were so many people; some had to stand up in the back of the sanctuary. It had to be over 300 people there because I was told the chapel's capacity and I'm sure we were way over. The funeral, the wake, and the repass were a blur for me. I was told later about all who had attended. People from my job were there, a few of Meco's former teachers, as well as other people that I was told had hugged me; but I do not remember.

CHAPTER 10

Feelings of Anger

Everyone came to my house after the repass. My entire street was full of people and cars lined up the cul-de-sac, road and driveway. I was still trying to keep my sanity by staying busy. I entertained company, I cleaned, I cooked.... I could not stop crying. I was starting to feel like I didn't want to live anymore. I felt like I needed God to remove just a little of the pain I was feeling so it wouldn't hurt so badly. I couldn't help but notice every time I would walk into a room people would stop talking and get very quiet. I knew there was some gossiping going on, but I just pretend not to notice. All the secrecy was making me even angrier! Everything made me angry, I was angry looking at the other mother's wishing their children a happy birthday on Facebook. I was angry about them talking about their accomplishments, when my child had been robbed of his. Although it sounds awful this is how I was feeling. You would not understand if you have not suffered from the loss of a child. I guess it is just a part of the phase you go through. I knew the anger that I felt surfacing would not lead to anything good, so I just continued to keep myself busy.

Finally, one of my cousins pulled me to the side to ask if I had talked to the people who were in the parking lot of the club. I told her I had spoken to them all, but no one saw the shooter. "No, she said. "I didn't want to know if they saw the shooter". I wanted to know if you've been told about what happened after he was shot?"she said. "No what happened!", I asked. She went on to tell me once Meco had been shot, someone told Mercedes she needed to take him to the hospital and she said, "I am not going nowhere without my f*@$in brother". She was referring to OG whom at this point they still had not found yet.

My cousin then went on to tell me that they asked why they were still in the parking lot after they had been kicked out of the club and she was told it was because Mercedes had gone back into the club. She said she had to use the restroom. They said it had taken her a while to come back out, so Nae had to go back inside to get her. When Nae went in to get her, she sees her on the dance floor dancing. That was not the end there was more. I was not sure if I could stand to hear anymore, my body felt like it was boiling on the inside. This is the last thing I need to tell you, my cousin said. I am not telling you this to hurt you, but I feel like you should know. I do not want you walking around in the blind and everyone else knows what's going on. She then said that while Nieya was on her way to drive Meco to the hospital Mercedes told her to pull into the Shell gas station, then she ordered a Lyft for her and KD to go home. I was so angry, as well as hurt at this point. I was ready to let everything go. I love my husband's children as if they were my own, but this was too much for me to cope with. My husband has been there for me every step of the way and I see how it is affecting him. But I am not sure if I can continue with the marriage when I did not want to have anything else to do with his child. I went upstairs alone and cried uncontrollably. I was already angry about Mercedes leaving Meco at the gas station to die once they got there; now there was more. I was not sure where this information was coming from and I was too upset to talk to Mercedes or my husband about it. I was hearing that several of my family members were very upset about it. This was not the time to cause a big altercation, so I had to let it go for now. Mercedes was gone home but my husband was there with me and I tried my hardest not to take my anger out on him.

My husband and I met at Fitzgerald Park in Tucker, Georgia where his son, Lil Ade and Meco both played football for the same team. I love him dearly, but feelings were all over the place. I felt guilty for being with, Ade and inside my head I beat myself up for believing that if I had not been with Ade, maybe this would not have happened. Meco would not have been at that club. It was weird because I also felt guilty for feeling this way. I know I could not make it through such a tough and trying time without my husband by my side. I was also angry with some of my family members because they were spreading the anger, telling other family members what they heard Mercedes had done instead of them trying to find out if it was true especially since I was not strong enough to do so. I was always the support and took the lead putting things together for the family; so why couldn't they figure this out for me instead of stirring the pot even more. Chico was a thin guy and Meco was built like him. I was mad that I had a child with someone so thin. Maybe if he had been thicker, it could have stopped the bullet from getting to his heart. I had allowed my hurt to turn into anger and I could not get it under control.

CHAPTER 11

Help Me Live

The day after the funeral my family packed up to go home. I was apprehensive about them leaving because I did not know how I would cope without them. I knew my husband would have to go back to work soon. He is a contractor; when he doesn't work, he doesn't get paid. My youngest two children, Mesha and Marco were the last two in school, they had been out for a week and would have to go back soon. My friends would be at work, so who would be there to help occupy my time and to help keep my mind off things. I was still on leave from school for another three weeks and work another two and a half months.

My husband and I have been sleeping on the couch for a little over two weeks. I still only went upstairs to brush my teeth, shower, and change clothes. I did not understand why I could not bring myself to sleep in my room (not that I was getting any sleep anyway). I could not seem to stay asleep for more than 2 hours at a time. My eyes would just open, sometimes full of tears. I would turn away from my husband and cry quietly trying not to wake him up with my muffled sounds. I held in my outbursts or sometimes I would go into the bathroom to try to let it out as quietly as I could. Ade went back to work a few days after my family members left and I was home alone. I tried to keep busy making business calls, but I could not focus. The tears would not stop flowing and my head began to hurt. I did not want to call my mom or any of my close family because I knew they were hurting too. I knew my best friend Charlene would be sleeping because she worked third shift. I stared at Meco's urn which sits on the floor in front of my fireplace next to my best friend Terrell's urn, who'd died a few years earlier in 2013. The more I got into my feelings the more my thoughts went astray. Why was God keeping me here to suffer? The other children would be better off here without me bringing them down. I would never be happy again. I needed to end this pain because it was too much for me. Why couldn't I lay here and die without having to kill myself. If I killed myself would my family and loved ones understand? They have no idea how unbearable this is. Suddenly, I just snapped out of my thoughts and I literally said out loud, "you have to get some help". I immediately went upstairs to get dressed. If I had not, I probably would not be here telling this story.

When I got into the car, I was not sure where I was going but I had to get out of the house. I googled the number to several psychologists. I began to call around; I needed an appointment ASAP. I was trying to get a walk-in appointment for that day. I needed to get help. I must have called five different offices to no avail. All I would get was a voicemail. I called Victims of Crime to see if they could refer me somewhere or if they had someone who could help me over the telephone right at that moment. I finally found a place on Google that accepts walk-ins, so I headed in that direction. When I got there the room was full of people and I approached the window to sign in. "Ma'am may I help you?" she said. With my eye's bloodshot red from crying for hours I told her I needed to speak to someone. She did not seem to have any concern about how bad off I was or if I could make it to the next day she simply said, "we are full for the day and cannot take anyone else". I just turned and walked away from the window; I headed back to the car before she was able to finish talking. When I got back to the car, I let out a loud yell as I began kicking and hitting the ceiling of the car. I hated that I was still alive. I had talked myself out of taking a handful of pills to end it all but here I sit with no one to help me. During my episode my phone rang, and it was Robert, a volunteer for Victims of Crime returning

43

my call. I told him what I was going through and how I was having a hard time getting some help.

Robert began talking to me, telling me his story. He offered to find a place for me to get the help I needed. Just being able to talk to someone and knowing that someone was there to help me find a psychologist to talk to it made me feel better. Robert was able to take a lot of the frustration away. Getting rid of this frustration calmed me down more than I could imagine. I was finally able to stop crying and drive home.

When I got home Dora, my nephew Buck's children's mother had made it to the house. Their daughter Malaya was only about 8 months old and she occupied my time for several days after my husband left for work. He did not start back going every day; he would stay at home with me every couple of days and I loved having his company. It was different for me because I am the type of person that is fine with being home alone. I do not get bored easily. There is always housework or some type of business I need to take care of but during this time; I needed people around me more than ever before. I had been hearing information about the person from the so-called "Blood gang" (as I was told they called themselves) that was at the club that night. They considered themselves rappers and would perform at different clubs in the area. This is one of the performances that Meco and everyone else thought they were going to. An open mic night for one of Mercedes' friends which neither of them end up seeing that night. I would tell the detective where they were supposed to be, I would send her pictures, give nicknames and any other information I found out about them, but still, no one was arrested.

My anger was becoming unbearable because it was now November and none of them have been arrested. I spoke to the news a few times and they began getting tips from the Crime Stopper telephone line, but the detective kept saying she could not disclose a lot of information. This pissed me off even more. If she would just give me a bit of information; I would be able to use it to find out more.

This did not make any sense to me, maybe she did not know as much as she pretended to, maybe it was like the boys said in the beginning, "they had a whole different agenda". My anger was overwhelming, so I decided to take the law into my own hands. They would not get away with what they've done even if my life had to end to get it done.

Robert had found a psychologist for me but at the time he called I needed him for a different reason. It was no longer to stop me from ending my own life but to stop me from ending the life of those responsible for my son's death. My emotions were all over the place; the sadness, the pain, and the guilty feelings had now turned to anger and revenge. I got in the car and drove to a location that the "Blood gang boys" frequented. I had studied the pictures of the group so I would be able to know their faces if I was to see them. I would be able to call the police immediately but today; the memory of their faces was not for the same purpose. My mind was made up; if one of the people came out, I was going to take their life as they had done to my son. After sitting there for about two hours my phone rang, it was my husband, "where you at?" he asked. It was as if he had been home and had not seen me there however, he was at work. I told him where I was, and he told me to "please go home and do not ever do that again". I could not argue with him. Even though, it felt like killing them would make me feel better; I knew I was wrong. Deep down inside I know it would not make me feel any better. I started the car and went home.

The next week I went to my first therapy appointment. Although, it was only my first one-hour appointment I felt a little relief because I finally found a therapist. The therapist gave me a lot to think about such as the anger I was harboring with some family members. It made me rethink what I had been told about the things Mercedes said and done that night. One of the main things I thought about was the statement she allegedly made about taking Meco to the hospital. I did not like her choice of words; nor did I like the actions she took that night. However, when I put myself in her shoes, I can empathize with her. If one of my brothers had been shot and my other brother was somewhere laid out from being badly beat; I would not have left neither of them.

I know I need so much more therapy because I still have so many questions and feelings of anger against the world. The only thing that was going to help me get rid of some of the anger is to get answers to these questions that are floating around in my head. I needed to know why they were still in the parking lot. I wanted a breakdown of the time frame of that night. I wanted to know everything that happened in full detail.

CHAPTER 1 2

The Blame Game

After attending a few therapy sessions; I began to cry less and less. I was also starting to get a little sleep. I feel like I am finally getting some of the answers to the questions I been battling with. While speaking to a few of the guys that were at the club that night; I came to find out the shooting did not occur until 20 minutes after Mercedes had already come out of the club. I also came to find out Dre, Niq, and JJ were trying to go inside the club knowing it was a club full of "Bloods". I also learned that the security guard was still going to let them inside even after the incident transpired with them trying to fight Meco. I was told Mercedes start yelling and pushing them back demanding him not to allow them to go back inside of the club. She got into an argument with the security guard for agreeing to let them in.

I reached out to my cousin JJ, to get some answers "I am going to be honest with you Meka, if we would have gone back inside the club it would have been more casualties because those guys were obviously not trying to talk,". Hearing this made me mad with JJ, Niq, and Dre, I did not understand how the three of them thought they would be able to talk to a large group of people that were being violent with every group of guys that came in the club. They said all they were trying to do was calm the situation. I feel like pride stepped in the way; that is why no one told me what was going on when they walked out the door. I was still angry and now it has been redirected towards the guys in the family, who were out there. They were trying to handle the situation like boys instead of men which resulted in Meco's death.

I still would feel guilty whenever I laughed or had a decent day. I found a way to blame everyone that was at the club that night. I even found a way to blame myself. If only I had run out of the house immediately and followed the guys to the club. If only I had stayed on the phone with Meco until he drove out of the parking lot. My thoughts were still all over the place and the questions in my head were only making the blame shift even more. I was mad about everything! Some of my earlier thoughts resurfaced, why I had I not chosen a thick guy to have children with, maybe the bullet would not have travel through. What if I had married a man and the only children we had were biologically both of ours; would things have been different? I was told Meco went to the club because his girlfriend, Nae decided to go. I found myself blaming him being in a relationship with her. I knew in my mind that I needed to stop blaming everyone and everything for his death. I received a call from the detective giving me several details about that night. She told me the group was known for gang activity and there were seventy plus people with these guys from the club. She also let me know that there were over one hundred shell casings found in the parking lot of the plaza. All from several different guns, so it was hard to tell which gun or bullet killed Domiquo. This saddened me because I was not sure what this would mean regarding to the right person being arrested for his murder. What evidence would they have to make sure the right person is found guilty? The thought of this made me nauseous.

When I hung up the phone tears immediately began to fall. I came to the realization that his time on earth was up and there was nothing I could do about it. There were over one hundred gunshots that night. Meco and one other person were the only people that were hit. She was shot in the leg while my second-born son died that night. He was the only one that died out of over ninety people in that parking lot; his death was an act of God. How do you get through something like this, something that hurts so bad and is just so hard to accept?

Was God paying me back for something? I try to help others as much as I can; I am honest, fair, and God-fearing. I can't understand why something so awful has happened to me. They say, "all things work for the good of those who love the lord". I love the Lord; I pray to him regularly; what kind of lesson can come out of me losing a child. Did I deserve this?

Sitting and thinking one day I decided I was finally through playing the blame game. I concluded that God needs good people on his team too and Meco made it to the best team he could ever be on. I am still not sure what good could possibly come out of this situation. Then thoughts of how Meco lived his life came to mind. How he was a role model to so many. Meco's brothers and sisters, as well as some of the other children in the neighborhood, mentioned how he would get on them and correct them whenever they weren't behaving appropriately. There was a bigger battle and God needed him as a foot soldier to help him fight. He needs someone who will help save the lives of other youth and young adults that need the whisper of an angel to lead them in the right direction. God decided my son, Meco, was the best one for the job and there was no better person in that parking lot that night, for this job.

Even if he had not died in the parking lot that night, it was still his time to rest. It hurt so bad to come to this realization. It was so much easier to have someone to blame, somewhere to deflect my anger. I needed something to focus my mind on besides the fact that I will never see my son again. I will never see him again in the flesh walking this earth. He'll never walk in the door calling out "ma".

The only one to blame was the people who were responsible for ending his life so abruptly. The Gwinnett County Police station had the security guard in custody because he started the shooting but there were still others responsible for starting the altercation in the club.

CHAPTER 13

The News Coverage

While sitting in the living room watching television a short clip about Domiquo's incident flashed as an upcoming news story. The story about Meco had not aired in a few days, so I was shocked to see it and immediately wondered what I was about to find out. The anticipation began to build up so to occupy my mind I made a phone call to my son Niq. I wanted to know if he had heard any new information, however, Niq did not answer. As soon as I hung up my phone rang; it was the detective. She said she wanted to speak with me before I saw the news story. The news I received from her had me stunned; I was in shock. They had arrested O'shay, also known as O'block. He was a kid my children and I had known since they were in elementary school. Questions began to run through my mind, "what part did he play in Meco's murder", "was Meco setup" I asked the detective. She advised that since they could not pinpoint who bullet shot and killed Meco; they were arresting and charging everyone who was shooting at the scene that night. Anyone could have been his killer. I had mixed emotions about the arrest. I did not think O'shay would do anything intentionally to hurt Meco, but the news also made me wonder if he had been the one to shoot the bullet that killed him. If O'shay was the killer, did he know that he had shot my son? So many questions rang through my mind. I needed to know what my children had heard about this. I began my search for more answers.

Here we go again I am receiving different stories about why O'shay was in the parking lot that night. The first story was O'shay's brother Tank had gotten into an argument with the same guys that were trying to fight with Meco. The other story was O'shay came to the club after seeing the message from the group text that read, pull up to Midnight Blu on Jimmy (which was short for Jimmy Carter Boulevard and bring the sticks. I was not sure which story was true, but I still had questions. Did anyone see O'Shay with a gun, if so, was he shooting and in what direction. Some of the children I asked said they did not see him there at all while others said they saw him in a car pull right up in front of the club. Others said they heard it was the car O'shay was in, but they did not see anyone get out. Some said gunshots came from the car and the shots were aimed towards the club. I heard some say where the car was parked there was no way O'shay could have shot Meco. I felt a sense of relief, but I was still very frustrated by this new information and all the different versions. I tried not to allow the anger to consume me all over again.

While lying on the couch with the television watching me, I received a phone call. Nae called to tell me O'shay's mother and sister would like to talk to me. They were upset about murder charges being brought up on him. "Ask them if it is okay for you to give me his mom's telephone number and I will give her a call," I said. Soon as Nae texted me the number I called it. When his mom answered the telephone, I told her who I was, her tone began to harden as she spoke. "O'shay would never do anything to hurt Meco so I don't understand why he was arrested for his murder. "He cried like a baby when he found out Meco was dead" she said. "I didn't know they were looking at him as a suspect or that they were going to arrest him until the detective called me today. I don't think O'shay would intentionally hurt Meco either", I said. With an even harder tone, "I heard you told the police to arrest everyone at the scene that was shooting. Someone told them O'shay was shooting so that is why he was arrested" she said. I evenly matched her tone because I was getting upset by the conversation, "whoever told you I said that is not making any sense, do you think the police are going to do what I tell them to do? I hated to hear your son was arrested and I hate that mine is no longer here but there is nothing I can do about either situation" I said. She went on to ask if I could tell them that he would not hurt Meco and how they had been knowing one another since elementary. I explained to her that I was not going to do or say anything that would upset the police department and jeopardize them doing what they need to do to solve Meco's case. I then suggested that she reach out to let them know why she did not feel like her son killed Meco. "They are not going to believe me; I am his mother"! They are just going to feel like I am saying he would not do it because of that" she said. "Well there is nothing I can do, my hands are tied", I said. Being that I had just lost my son, I was empathetic to any other mother that was in my position. Although her son wasn't dead, she too was in jeopardy of losing her son. This empathy helped me to handle the call in the manner that I did.

CHAPTER 14

Just Say No to Holidays

Thanksgiving was the first holiday that I had to make it through after Domiquo's death. I started to feel more depressed the days leading up to the holiday. My husband, Ade, the children and I decided to spend the holiday in Ohio with my family to occupy our time I was also not up to cooking or doing anything else for that matter. I remember waking up with tears in my eyes, so I quietly went to the bathroom to cry, trying not to ruin everyone else's holiday. I tried to collect my emotions quickly because I did not want anyone to notice me missing. My daughter, Mesha, was lying in my mom's bed sleeping. As soon as I lie next to her, I began to sob as quietly as possible. My body shook from the uncontrollable inner cry. My daughter reached over and rubbed my arm, but her eyes never opened. When she reached out to comfort me in her sleep it made me sob even more. I was gasping for air because I'd cried so much, I could barely breathe. I did not want to call out to my family members who were sitting downstairs talking, so I called my friend Nikki. I needed to try to talk this through; I needed to calm down.

Sitting in my mom's bathroom on the side of the tub with the telephone to my ear; I could barely get the words "hello" out of my mouth. When Nikki answered the phone, my breathing had become even shallower and my heart was racing. I dropped the phone to the floor and got on all fours trying to force air out of my body. Holding my mouth open did not seem to help. I could hear the panic in Nikki's voice, "where are you? Who's there with you? Can you call for someone to help you?" she yelled from the other end of the telephone.

I hated to put her in this situation, I could not get out words to tell her what was going on. I laid down on my back, stretching my neck out as far as I could trying to take in as much air as I could. Finally, I started to catch my breath. I let Nikki know I was okay as soon as I was able to talk again.

Once I calmed down, I talked to Nikki for a while and it helped me to calm down a little more. When I went back into the room with my daughter what she said next touched my heart. "Ma, did you hear me calling your name or feel me tapping your arm?" she said. "I felt you rub my arm but not calling my name, I looked at you when you touched my arm, but you were still sound asleep," I said. "I could see Meco standing in grandma's bedroom doorway, I could see you lying there crying and he told me to tell you to stop crying because he was okay. When I called your name, you would not answer me, so I tried tapping you on the arm to get your attention, but you still did not answer me," she said. This sent chills through my body, but I was glad to hear Meco was okay. I explained to her that she was not saying anything out loud; it was part of her dream. He came to her in the dream to give me that message and I was alright now. A few weeks before Meco's birthday; we decided to do a candlelight vigil and a balloon release. I had agreed to inform the First 48 of the next time we were getting together in Meco's honor. They were to come over to film the event. Everyone gathered at my house along with a producer and a camera person from the show. None of my other children wanted to be a part of the show but we finally got one or two of them to sit in, however, they refused to speak on camera.

My mom Carol, nephew Brandon, my husband and I sat in the living room answering questions and telling them what type of person Meco was. We told them about his younger years, his adolescent years, all the way up to the young adult he turned out to be. They filmed others in the house as well as the release of the balloons. I was in hopes all of this would aid in catching some of the other people responsible.

I was hoping someone would see this episode on the First 48 and call into crime stoppers with a helpful tip. I know the police were looking for two additional people; a young girl with white hair, whose name (I was told) was Ty'Rhianna and a guy with braids that I was not familiar with. The First 48 staff was very nice; they made us feel very comfortable talking to them. They stayed around and talked to us even after the cameras stopped rolling. It was as if they had known us personally. I thanked them for giving us the opportunity to share my son's story and they left letting me know they would be in touch.

Christmas was coming fast, and I was in fear of how I would get through this day. Not only was it, Christmas day but December 25th is also Domiquo's birthday. There had not been a birthday that I was not able to see his face. We always spent Christmas together as a family even if it was for half the day before they went to their dad's house or to hang out with friends. Meco loved home cooked food so he would always stand in the kitchen rubbing his hands together asking how much longer before the food would be done. I had not bought one gift yet and there were only two weeks left until Christmas. Mesha asked, when was I going shopping and I expressed that I did not care about or want to do anything for Christmas. All I wanted to do was sleep the day away. "You still have other kids ma, you act as if you died with Meco, we still here," she said. It hurt so bad to hear her say this. I knew I had to pull myself together... but it was so hard. The next day I forced myself to begin my Christmas shopping.

Although, it was something I truly did not want to do; I pulled myself out of bed on Christmas morning. I did this all for my two teenage children and my grandchildren who always came over so we could watch them open the gifts we bought for them. After they would open their gifts, as a family we would always help put together and show them how to operate the new toys. After the children play with their toys for a little while everyone would help clean up the wrapping paper. Then we would eat, relax and sit around talking. I tried to keep my composure as long as possible, but I could not take it anymore, so I eased towards the stairs because I needed to cry. The urgency to cry hit me quickly but I could not allow them to see me like this. Before I could reach the top of the stair's tears had already started falling from my eyes. They were filling up fast. I rushed to my room and locked my room door. I threw myself on top of my bed and I sobbed. I could hear the Christmas music playing downstairs and several voices were singing the song. I cried harder; how could they dare enjoy themselves on his day. He is not here to enjoy it. How could things be so normal for them, while I was hurting so bad.

There was a knock on my bedroom door, so I tried to clean up my face as much as possible but there was no hope. My eyes were bloodshot red, and I could not stop the tears from falling. When I opened the door, it was my son Ade and my son Marco; they knew I was having a hard time. They came to get me out of the room and to try to cheer me up. "I knew somebody was missing, I said where is my mom" said Ade. "Yeah, so we came to get you" said Marco. When I went downstairs, I could tell they had been crying down there as well. We all held it together as much as we could while waiting on this day to end.

The next day on December 26th; I received some great news. Detective Kulnis, who had been working hard on Domiquo's case, called to tell me they arrested Kyese. He was the main person I wanted to be sure was arrested because I was told he started the entire altercation. You know the guy that had popped Meco in the face with the bandana. They arrested him during his appearance at Dekalb County Courthouse for the Armed Robbery charges he was already facing. He refused, to answer any questions the detective had about Meco's murder and immediately asked for a lawyer. Detective Kulnis went on to apologize for not being able to arrest Kyese before Domiquo's birthday, I was so happy to hear she got him the specific day did not matter. The arrest was like music to my ears just knowing they had him in custody was a big relief to me. I had heard so much about him and none of it good. He needed to be off the streets.

CHAPTER 15

M.E.C.O.'s Joi

(Millions Everywhere Against Crime While Offering A Way Out w/ Joi)

I went back to work on January 2, 2018. I was not sure how I would be able to cope with sitting and looking at the computer all day while answering upsetting emails from sales reps and customers. Dealing with a new system I only had a short time to learn before I went on leave. I had been off for three months with so much on my mind that I was not sure I would remember how to maneuver through the new system. My job requires a lot of attention to detail so I was worried I would not be able to focus and would make a lot of mistakes.

When I walked into the office my co-workers were very welcoming. Several of them had stayed in touch with me during my time of need and even came over a few times to visit. They were a great part of my support system and I truly appreciated them. Talking to my coworker/friend, Felecia, had been very therapeutic because she'd experienced the loss of her daughter a few years prior. She understood the emotional turmoil I was going through. She helped me talk things out several times over the telephone and on her visits to my house. My friend, Nikki, worked with me as well, she had been a great supporter from the beginning. My friend Sherri was always so attentive to me and full of positive energy. Then I had

Ebony who is very kind-hearted and always did or said things to help lift my spirits. She is like a natural comedian so she would make me laugh at times when I did not think I had the energy to do so.

I had been back to work for a while now and it was going fairly well. I remembered more of the system than I thought I would, and it felt good to get out of the house. It felt good to know I had a strong support system at home and away. You never know when you are going to have a breakdown or start crying uncontrollably, but I knew that if that happened, I had these four people there to help me get it back together.

I often wondered what my calling in life is. What is it that God wants me to do to serve him? What was I put on this earth to do? The thought made me think back to the things I had gone through in my life. I have suffered the loss of several close relatives not only had I lost my granddad Wesley, aunt Rebecca, first cousin Ricky, my ex Ced and my best friend Terrell but I had also lost my father Lucius, sister Diane, and now my son, Meco. I was fondled as a child and because of this I subconsciously made several bad decisions when it came to my choice in men. I was unable to trust men during my adult life. That was not all I had gone through. I was also a cancer survivor. I suffered from Cervical and Pelvic Cancer which resulted in radiation five days a week and chemotherapy one day a week for six months. The cancer was not in a place that could be surgically removed however I had to have a few surgeries so the radiation could effectively reach the cancer. The only conclusion I could come up with once I looked back on all the pain I've been through; is that God allowed me to go through all these things so I could know first-hand how to help others cope with these types of situations. I would know what other basic needs would be in these situations so I could provide or lead them to the resources they need in order to make it through such a tough time in their life.

A situation my oldest son Niq had gone through with a close friend of his entered my thoughts. His friend, Majic had gotten into a situation with the law which resulted in his death while in custody of the police. I remembered the young adults in the neighborhood trying to put their money together to pay for a funeral service for him. There were no government service available to help his family because he had prior felonies. I could not even imagine losing a child and not being able to send them home properly. That would be unbearable.

I now know my calling; I am here to help others cope with the turmoil in their life. I am a living testimony that even when you don't think you can make it, you can! Where would I start? Who would I start with? What would the name be? So many thoughts began to cloud my mind at once. I quickly picked up a notebook and a pen because I could not allow these thoughts to slip away.

I decided to start a nonprofit organization in honor of my son Meco. I needed to try to stop any other mother from experiencing such a loss. If they find their selves having to deal with such a tragedy, I do not want them to have to deal with it alone. Something people do not realize is even though you have family and friends to help you put your love one to rest and cope afterwards; they are the last ones you want to bother. You know and understand they are hurting as well. Being that Meco's life was taken due to violence; I decided to focus on reducing the crime rate. Our youth and young adults need to be given a positive outlet they can enjoy. They need to understand how important it is to graduate from High School and not just because their parents or society say they should. We will assist them in accessing the confidence and skills they need to get them on the right career path or become an entrepreneur. Meco's Joi would then need to help them sustain financially by giving them the skills to properly set goals, make good financial and life decisions that will decrease the feeling that they need to steal or commit other crimes to get what they want. The learning environment will be hands-on, and we will work on specific things in each individual's life that they would like to accomplish. This will allow them to see results at the end that benefit them. I could be more than just a help to our youth. I could be a companion to those suffering a loss; I could help make funeral plans as I hate to be able to say I have done more than once. When the organization grows, I can help pay for some of the funeral expenses for those who cannot afford to do so. I also wanted to provide financial assistance for everyday living needs and counseling for those who suffer from terminal illnesses. As I jotted these things down in my notebook, more thoughts began to pour into my scrambled brain. I looked up and thank God for his guidance.

After writing down the many ideas and ways I could help others; I needed to come up with a name. What happened with Meco was the final straw. I had always helped the children around the neighborhood fill out FASFA forms, feeding them, letting them stay over when they had nowhere else to go, taking them back and forth to sports games and practices so they could be involved in positive events. I needed to do more on a larger scale. I'd watched children who were barely attending school because of their circumstances go on to finish and stay out of trouble after they started spending time at my house with myself and my children. I know I can help make a difference by helping to increase the graduation rate while reducing the crime rate. I know I can do it.

I decided to use the acronyms for Domiquo's nickname, Meco but I needed the words I decided to use to be meaningful. I started jotting down several words that fit the acronym, but they were not powerful enough. I need the words to include all people. I finally came up with the words that would cover the action and the outcome I am striving for. The organization's name would be Millions Everywhere Against Crime While Offering A Way Out with Joi. I planned to cater to different needs; Crime and education while the other part of the organization focuses on companionship. We would offer companionship to those suffering from a loss as well as to those suffering from a terminal illness. Now that the name was in place, I needed a team to turn this tragedy into triumph. I began to reach out to those I knew I could trust and who naturally enjoyed helping people. I asked my friend Sherri, who I had not known very long but seemed like I had known her forever, to be the President of the foundation, Nikki, who I knew I could trust, to be my Treasure, Felecia, who had already helped me cope with so much of what I was going through, to serve as a consumer advocated which was great because she was attending school for her Masters in Social Work. Ebony, who was always getting people together at the job to feed the homeless, to give out book bags, and do other things in the community. She already had the drive to help others, so I decided to ask her to join the board of the foundation as the secretary.

Mercedes, my stepdaughter, was one of the first people I spoke to about starting the organization. She mentioned that she had spoken to Neil and Will, two of Meco's friends about them wanting to do something similar. They wanted to find a way to help with the youth in society and make a change.

They were eager but not sure how or where to start. She was enthusiastic and excited to help, so we began to discuss ideas and set up meetings with the others. Kiki, my other stepdaughter, Nieya, Meco's ex-girlfriend, and Diona one of their friends wanted to help with the organization also. They have all been standing strong and still doing their part. We started the organization on April 21, 2018, having our first barbeque. My sister, sons, nephews, and their friends have been very supportive as well. This was not only a way to honor Meco, but it was a way to give our family something that would bring us all closer together while we try our best to heal.

There are a lot of us that help others but there is so much more that can be done. There are different ways people can help and it does not always have to be financial. Sometimes help can mean so much more when you give some of your time. It can also be helpful to others when you offer them to utilize your skills. Although, several of us can do so much more we don't. I beg you! Please do not wait until something drastic happen in your life before you decide to be a part of something or before you decide to help others. It is not all about what you have it is what you do with what you do have. Invest your time and energy within your community around you as if you were doing it for your loved ones or the inside of your house. I'm sure together we can all make an impact.

CHAPTER 16

The First 48

While standing at Ebony's desk, she asked when the episode of the First 48 would air. It had been a few months since they'd filmed the episode and when she asked me it reminded me, I needed to reach out to them. Thinking about it made me anxious to see what they had put together. I wanted to see what was said during the interviews with the people involved that lead to who was arrested.

I quickly went back to my desk to call the producer of the show. That's when I came to find out she was no longer working with First 48. She gave me the contact information for the new producer. This concerned me; she is the one I told all the detailed information about Meco and what happened that night. How would the next producer pick up where she left off? What story would they tell? Having heard this news made me even more anxious to see the episode.

I called the current producer to find out if there was a date for the episode to air. It had been almost a year since they filmed at my house. The producer advised me they were still editing the episode and they would give me a call back within a day or so.

The second week of January I received a call from the new producer of First 48. She informed me the episode was set to air on February 7, 2019 at 8:30 pm on the A&E network. I quickly began to spread the word by posting it on my Facebook page, calling and texting friends and family to let them know to tune in. I was not sure if I would be able to watch the episode because I knew from watching past episodes, they would show the person's deceased body lying on the ground. I could not bear to see him lying there lifeless with only a sheet covering him. I also have not been able to watch him alive on videos yet. I am only able to look at pictures of him without breaking down. The show told me I would receive five compact disks of the episode for me to keep. I checked the mailbox everyday hoping I could have someone view the episode before it was viewed by the world, but I never received them.

February 7th came faster than I could imagine. I had decided I would listen to the episode because I knew I would not be able to watch it. I wanted to hear what the detective would reveal about how she found out her information. I also wanted to hear the interviews of the suspects involved. Nikki was coming over for emotional support. She arrived around 7:30 pm she brought chicken, pizza, and soft drinks with her. To my surprise a good friend of mine name Denise came with her along with her daughter Tasha. I was happy to see her because it had been a while since we'd seen one another. Denise has been very supportive of Meco's Joi. Later, my longtime friend, Reese, and her daughter, Nene, who is like a niece to me, came over. I was nervous and anxious about listening to the episode. This was going to be hard, but I wanted to hear what was said and how the investigation was handled.

Everyone except for my sons' Marco and Ade, said they would not be able to watch the episode. Shortly before the episode came on everyone else began to eat dinner but I had no appetite at all. In fact, my stomach was turning and the closer it got to 8 pm the higher my anxiety level rose. My anxiety was through the roof! We all settled in the living room where I sat in the recliner with my back to the television. Hearing them say, "nineteen years old victim Domiquo Riley" made my heart drop. I could not believe that after watching the show for so many years, it was my child they were talking about. My friends who were there knew my main objective was to find any information that I could elaborate on to help the case. I also wanted to see a picture of the other two people the police have not caught.

Thank God for this new age TV where we can pause and rewind any episode at any time. When the episode got to certain scenes, they would pause, the video and discuss what was going on during specific scenes.

Very early on I began to get upset with the First 48 because they made Meco's murder seem as if it was because he had some involvement with gangs. The only ones involved in a gang were the ones pursuing him. When the guys walked up in Meco's face there was a guy about 10 feet away from Meco with a blue and white shirt on and Meco hand was in the air as well. We paused on that scene too as we looked closely to see if they had thrown up any gang signs as someone on the episode had mentioned. The guy hands looked like he was throwing up a gang sign but Meco's hand was simply up in the air in a dancing motion as we had seen him do several times prior.

I asked Marco and Ade, who was watching the episode as well, if they knew the guy who was throwing up gang signs? They said they'd never seen him before. I know he did not ride there with Meco and noticed when the promoter parted them from the other guys, he was not near them. The only person, Terri pushed back with Meco was his stepbrother, OG. Looking at Meco standing there with the screen frozen although, I could barely see his face; it still made my heartache. The shirt he had on was a blue button-down bandanna print shirt, which did not seem like a big deal to me because I did not know of Gwinnett County being a gang area. Meco had left out the house several times with bandannas wrapped around his head to match his outfits. I knew how much he was into fashion and liked to look good. He did not discriminate about wearing any color. He wore red, blue, even pink and purple; it was not about looking hard or being a part of something it was about what looked good to him.

As the episode continued, they were not concentrating on the club scene anymore. I was upset because it was not even over and so much had been left out. There was so much that happened at the club that they did not show. They did not show what happened in the parking lot. Some of the footage was not completely clear but there was some camera footage. What about how the shooting started? How the guys were jumping on OG and beating him over the head with a Hennessy bottle. The detective had even told me Meco had jumped out of the car and ran around it towards the crowd where the fight was ensuing when he was shot. So why is it being portrayed as if Meco was fighting. The people in the car with Meco said he was never fighting anyone that night. That was me fighting ma not Meco, they got us confused. I jumped out of the car when I saw that it was OG who was getting jumped and started fighting, said Marco.

Meco and Marco are built very much alike; they are both over six feet tall and very slender. Their complexion is also the same so I understand how the mix up could happen.

They showed the text message on the episode sent in the group text that read "pull up and bring the sticks" and stated the text came from Meco; it made me angry with him, but I had to be realistic about it. He was a young man who had just been violated and hit in the face with a bandanna for absolutely no reason at all. I was able to watch the interviews in the police department while being very cautious not to see any of the clips of Meco lying on the ground deceased. The first interview of the young man whose face they did not show made me wonder who he was. He had given the detective so much helpful information. I wanted to reach through the television and give him a big hug.

It takes a lot of courage for young men and women to come forward nowadays. There's a sick notion that if you witness someone being hurt or killed; that it's not cool, to say anything to the police. They call it "snitching". I was so glad to see that this young man stood up for what was right regardless of what society says. He handled the situation in a way he would have wanted someone to do for one of his loved ones. It takes so much more courage to go against what society says is right versus doing what you know is right. That day he made the decision a man would have made instead of a boy that wanted to fit in and I truly appreciate it.

Watching the interview of the security guard sent a chill through my body. His soul seemed so cold. The way he behaved in his interview made my skin boil. Every time he laughed with such an arrogant attitude, it made me want to physically cause harm to him. I wanted to hawk spit in his face which is something I have always considered to be one of the most disgusting things you could do to a person.

How dare he laugh and act as if he is untouchable. I wanted to walk out of the room but hopes of seeing the interviews of the others charged kept me in my seat. Shortly after this thought it was announced that Kyese, one of the others charged, refused to say anything. The only thing he stated was that he was not at the club on the night of the incident.

This pissed me off even more, but it could be helpful to the case. He was seen on video in the club, his picture was on the flyer for the party that night, and on social media. He had also been pointed out as one of the shooters. My friends could see how upset I was becoming; they were upset as well but they tried to point out the good points. The episode mentioned how Domiquo had never been in trouble before. They said, he seemed to be a good young man but was at the wrong place at the wrong time.

CHAPTER 17

After the First 48

Going back to work the day after The First 48 aired Meco's story was very difficult. I had so much on my mind, it was hard to concentrate. I had to take it one day at a time. I'm sure my coworkers were going to have a lot of questions for me. They all know what type of child Domiquo was and this tragedy was puzzling to all.

Once I settled in at work, everyone was very quiet, so I decided to break the ice. "What did you think about the show last night?" I asked to no one in particular. Some began to tell me how it seemed as if parts of the story were missing. The show left everyone with many unanswered questions: What was the age requirement to get into the club, was there a Gwinnett County police officer on duty. They also wondered if the club promoter knew it was a "gang" party. They also asked about the video recording from the parking lot, and rather or not it could be used to catch the killer/killers. I tried to answer their questions as best as I could. The one thing I am sure of is that there were not any Gwinnett County police officers on duty. If there had been, things would've been handled differently. In my heart, I believe my son would still be here today if a police officer was on duty that night.

When I looked back at the pictures of Kyese and his group of friends, they always posed with their hands up, forming gang signs.

They'd have red bandannas hanging from their pockets, tied around their heads, or they would be swinging them in the air.

What amazed me most is when I saw my children's barber in the picture with Kyese and his friends. He had been the boys' barber since they were young boys. He is also the promoter that sold the tickets to the party that night. I was told the club was a twenty-one and over club but the security guard (the one that's being charged with Meco's murder) allowed them to pay extra money to get in. Majority of the people that were with Meco were under the age of twenty-one. I went on to tell them about some of the things that were left out of The First 48 episode. These were things that I felt were very important. I understand the show was only an hour-long, but there were some parts that should not have been left out.

We then discussed my anger towards the security guard for his arrogance he displayed on the First 48 episode. The way he laughed and acted cocky as if it was all a joke. We also discussed how I was upset that Meco had sent the group text that night. As we talked and went through the events of that night, I had to admit most young men or women would have been upset and they probably would have wanted to fight as well. Anyone of us could have allowed our pride to get in the way. This was a case of a young man being bullied who then stood up for himself. How did an event that seemed so minuscule turn deadly in a matter of minutes?

I received a lot of support when I posted on Facebook about The First 48 episode. Several people sent their condolences and expressed how they could tell that The First 48 had left out a lot. Some also encouraged me not to let the show get me down. They also mention they could tell the story was put together to boost ratings. I joined an online group called "Build a Sista Up" because I was broken and felt the need to have my spirit lifted. I also hoped to meet like mind women who had possibly gone through the pain of losing a child. Only someone who had lost a child could understand the turmoil I was going through inside. The First 48 episode left me feeling very upset and unsettled. I was beginning to regret giving them permission to do an episode about my son's case.

Several people in this group, as well as some of my co-workers, encouraged me to stay positive and not let the episode upset me. They reminded me it was only a TV show and it was their job to sensationalize things in order to boost their ratings. They went on to say, "anyone and everyone that knew Meco could look at his face and see the innocence in him". I was so thankful for the reminder and positive remarks because I had begun to forget the bigger picture. It was not about this tv show, it was about Meco and finding his killer. I had to admit they did make me feel better, but the way the episode portrayed him was tarnishing my son's image. He was always known to be a respectable and responsible person. The way the First 48 portrayed my son during the episode was not him. I refuse to allow, them or anyone else to distort my son's image!

April 2019, I went to Alabama to help my sister move. While I was in the house doing a telephone training for Meco's Joi I overheard a conversation beginning about Domiquo's death. I am not sure why or how such a conversation began but I seemed to be purposely excluded from it. The conversation seems to have continued for a while. I had time to finish the end of my training, take a shower, and throw on some clothes. I did not bother to inquire about the conversation because my ride was on the way. I was preparing to leave out with my cousin Latrease.

The next morning, I received a phone call from a family member whose name I do not care to mention. We discussed various events that were going on in the family. I then asked if Meco's death was part of the discussion I overheard the previous day. I already knew the answer. I also knew the rumors that were going around surrounding his death. I was so angry! It was a lowdown thing to bring up, especially when things were just starting to get back to some type of normalcy. The next few words pierced my ears like a knife. "Domiquo's killing was gang related, he wore a shirt he knew was gang affiliated. Snoop wore the same shirt at a live concert, and he is a known gang member. Some of the people Domiquo hang around call themselves being in a gang". I was pissed off. "How do you know anything about Domiquo? You live all the way in Alabama and didn't talk to him on a regular basis. Haven't you ever seen people you knew was not gang affiliated walking around in bandanna print shirts?". Did they not know how much Meco was into fashion?

This is just more of the aftermath from the First 48 episode due to how they portrayed things and how he was made to look. I went on to mention how Meco would mock and make fun of people that called themselves being in a gang. He would laugh at them for their stupidity and he would openly express his dislike. He did not hang with anyone on a regular basis besides his ex-girlfriend, Nieya and recently his new girlfriend, Nae. Our immediate family would often talk about him not being a follower and having a mind of his own. How he rode along and would often refuse his brothers or sisters when they would try to ride with him. Domiquo was different in many ways; normally when most teens get their driver's license they love to drive, especially when they get their first car but not Meco. Meco had become close with a young man named Nick who often drove Meco around in his own car. It was normal to see Meco's car pull up, with Meco, Nae, and Nick in it. They would get out and talk for a while then they would be on their way. Meco and Nae would also spend a lot of time at the house as well as at her mom's house. They would have the music playing and seemed to be having a ball; just the two of them. The family member tried to cut me off several times, but I would not stop talking. I yelled over them while in tears because they had to know what type of person Meco was. They had to know how responsible he was and how he was against the foolishness that being in a gang represented. I had to get all of this off my chest, If I hadn't, it was a good chance I would not speak to this family member for a long time, if ever again. The call ended abruptly, and I was full of anger, but it was time to end the conversation, at least for now.

When my sons, Marco, Niq, Ade, my nephew Buck, and Marco's friends arrived in Alabama to help with the move, I had to ask them if they had ever heard of Meco being involved in a gang. I was mad at myself for feeling like I needed to ask this question, but I had to be real with myself. Children can act one way in front of their parents but be a totally different person in the streets. My children have always been open with me, so I knew that was not the case. We talk about a lot of things you would never imagine a child telling a parent; I could not see there being that much of a difference. I asked them all as we stood out in front of my sister's house and in unison they answered "nawl not Meco". They wanted to know who would say something like that. They knew whoever said it must not have known Meco very well; if they did that thought would have never crossed their mind. I agreed with them. Niq began to tell me how upset he was with The First 48 for saying Meco sent the text to the group that read "bring the sticks". "Meco is not the one who sent that message, he said. I was in shock that was the first time I was told that the message did not come from him. It was a big relief! They were starting to get upset from the accusations about Meco, so I told them let's just get back to moving; we carried on.

Against my better judgement, I logged into Facebook and joined the First 48 Fan page. The First 48 TV crew came out on March 23, 2019 to film the "Family Day" event for Meco's Joi Foundation. Therefore, I wanted to check out the page to see how their Facebook page would differ from the actual TV show. My mind began to wonder about what people may have commented about the episode. As I scrolled through the posts, searching for the date the episode aired…I could feel my heart pounding through my chest. For some reason, I was full of anxiety. The anxiety soon turned into anger after reading only the first few comments. I could not believe some of the comments that I was reading. I was appalled…

Some were saying how the episode about Meco's case was boring. That confused me…How do you find a true story about someone's loved one being killed boring? Did they realize this is a true story and not something that is being made up or meant to be sensationalized? This was not a story set out to entertain someone. I went on to read a few more comments. As I scrolled down, I read a post that said, "the kid would be alive if he had not called rival gang members". I was so mad tears began to fall from my eyes. I could not continue to just read any longer. I had to comment. I needed everyone to realize that their child could one day end up in this situation.

Thoughts were going through my head faster than I could type them; my fingers were shaking. I had to let these people know that my son was not in a gang. The First 48 show had left so much information out of the episode. So, once again, I found myself on the defense, explaining to others the true/real story. I waited for someone to respond so I could jump in and scorch their eyes out with my words. I usually take pride in not cursing or having a foul mouth but today was a different day. Today I was mad; I wasn't sure what would come out of my mouth or the tips of my fingers. While waiting for someone to comment about my son; I received a notification from the page from someone I knew. It was from my cousin Latrease. I was not aware that she was a member of the First 48 Facebook page. She sent a post to me and it was right on time. It was full of encouragement and thoughtful words at a time when I truly needed it. Latrease lost her child, LaRaven Jakeara, when she was only 3 months old. So, I knew she understood exactly how I was feeling. Reading the encouraging post from my cousin made me realize I had to turn away from the nonsense; I closed Facebook and found something more productive to do.

CHAPTER 18

What's Next

My life has been changed forever. It has been almost two years since Domiquo Mauriquez Riley was taken from us. Sometimes I still break down like it was yesterday.

Holidays were hard the first and second year after Meco's death but then some were not as hard while others only got harder. My birthday was harder for me than his. I was missing one of the Happy Birthdays I had heard for several years. Soon as I opened my eyes that morning tears started to cover my face. I tried not to sniffle too loud and control my body from shaking, but it was out of my control. His birthday was easier because it is on Christmas day and everyone is around which occupies your time, although it does not take your mind off it. My husband must have felt the uncontrollable shaking; he pulled me close to him and put his arm around me. I still could not stop myself from crying.

I miss feeling his long arms wrapping around me, with his clean smell, fresh haircut and nice gear. I miss him rubbing his hands together in the kitchen as he waits on his home-cooked meal. Sometimes I feel like lying in my bed until my eyes do not open anymore; just so I could see him again, but I know my other children and grandchildren need me. Meco would also want me to figure out what's next because everyone in the family was used to me being a happy person; a person who was always planning the next move. My grandmother, Julia is ninety-four years old and there had never been a family reunion just for her to include our entire family. Me and my children did a lot to make this a wonderful event for her. A small group of family members helped decorate, lift furniture, load and unload tons of items, while the others pitched in financially; she really enjoyed it. Meco was on the front line helping and complaining along with my other boys. I could not imagine putting another reunion together without him. My husband and I had gotten all our children and grandchildren together to take a family picture and it turned out nice. At this point I do not know if I would be able to take a family picture without him in it. What do you say when people ask you how many children do you have? My normal response was easy I would simply say we have nine. Then I would break it down for them stating, I have four and my husband has five. What do I say now? I would not dare say eight as if he never existed. My new normal is to say, we have nine children, but we lost one in October 2017. You do not ever really stop to think about things like this that seem so little while going on with your daily life. When you lose a child, you think about things like this often. One thing I must do from day to day is to continue to work on me and figure out how I can try to be happy while living my new normal.

What's next for me is to be there for my other children, my husband, my mom, my nephews and my sisters as they cope with the loss of our loved one. Hugging one another as a part of our greeting and telling each other I love you before we leave.

My children and my nephews are like brothers and sisters. They have always been very close. My oldest son has been the one that I have noticed taking Meco's death the hardest. When he calls me crying, I fight back my tears just long enough to make it through the call. Then I hang up and cry, like a baby. I know it is okay for us to cry together but when he sees me hurting, it will only make him more upset. You learn to cope with your children according to their ability to cope. That is something I have learned while on this journey.

What's next for me is to make sure everyone remembers Domiquo for the person he truly was and to not allow his death to be in vain. I always talk to Meco, when I pray, I tell him how much I love and miss him; just as I did when he was physically here with me. The birth of the nonprofit foundation, M.E.C.O.'S Joi (Millions Everywhere Against Crime w/ Joi), gave me a way to still perform a motherly duty for my son. I am in the process of nurturing and growing and caring for this foundation. I am building this foundation to have a heart of gold just like his. He was a great role model and I want to build up thousands more like him. He had a 401k plan at the age of nineteen; I would like thousands more to follow in his footsteps. That is why Meco's Joi teach youth and young adults about financial literacy, decision making, and goal setting. When he owed a debt, he made sure to budget his money so he would be able to pay it back. He also made sure to always pay his car note and his portion of the insurance on time. It's time for me to not only hug my own loved ones but to show love to other children and young adults who may feel as if no one loves or cares about them.

What's next for me is to give back for all that God has done for me. To give back for the nineteen years he allowed me to spend with Domiquo. Give back for waking me up every morning, even those mornings when I didn't feel like waking up. I want to give other people the knowledge and encouragement that they can be successful in life no matter the hand they are dealt.

A Letter to My Son

Rest in heaven Domiquo Mauriquez Riley you will always be loved and never forgotten. Although you were here for only a short period of time; you truly left your mark on this world.

Please come and pay me a visit; it doesn't matter if I am asleep or awake. Let me feel your presence and the feeling of your arms wrapped around me. Say the word "ma" in my ear every now and then; I just want to hear your voice. We left the service for your phone on with your voicemail on it so we can hear your voice. Sometimes it is so painful that I hang up before the voicemail starts but other times I smile when I hear your voice. Send me a sign to let me know you hear me when I talk to you.

Ask God to help us make sure that justice is served for you and Peeper, rather it is jail time or by life slowly punishing them. Ask him to help our cousin, Tiffany out of the horrible situation that she's in. Make sure you watch over her while she completes whatever this mission is God has her on. Buck and a young lady name Krista you did not get to meet had a baby and they decided to give him your name as a middle name; Kayson Domiquo. Several people in the family got shirts and tattoos with your name and/or picture on it. Big Mac opened a club, he has your name written on the wall in graffiti and he also had a 3D image of you made. I guess I am telling you all this to let you know that you were loved by many, but I don't have to because I know you are watching over us and already see it all.

Do your best work as an angel and as a soldier in the army of the Lord. Be sure to cover, protect, and shield your family while in heaven as you would have here on earth.

I Love and Miss you! Sincerely your Mom.

The Story of Ricky Julious

In 1984 Ricky "Peeper" Julious was born; Peeper was the nickname given to him as a small child. Ricky was a preemie at birth with NAS, the acronym for Neonatal Abstinence Syndrome. According to the medical encyclopedia, NAS is a group of conditions caused when a baby withdraws from certain drugs he's exposed to in the womb before birth. When these drugs are taken by the mother during pregnancy, they can pass through the placenta and cause serious problems for the baby.

I am very close to my mom's brother, my Uncle Ricky, who is Peeper's father. The first time I saw Peeper; I instantly fell in love with him. All I saw was this tiny frail body with all these tubes hooked up to him; He had the littlest club feet. I knew right then he was a fighter.

In 1987 I was living with my elderly grandmother, helping her out. Peeper's mom came over and asked if I could watch him until she came back. He was 3 years old at that time; she never returned. That's when I took on the responsibility of raising him along with my grandma. Peeper was my first baby. He was a quick learner; I taught him his daily prayers, sent him to school, volunteered on school field trips, I cooked for him and ran his bathwater. Oh, how I loved him. I didn't give birth to him, but I loved and cared for him just like he was my own.

For most of his life, Peeper was raised in the Village of Lockland, Ohio. When he became an adult, he remained a resident there. Peeper and his pregnant girlfriend, Denise and her 2 children made Lockland their home also. On April 20, 2016, she gave birth to Peeper's second son, Ricky Lee Julious Jr., Peeper was so happy to have another son.

On March 22nd, 2017; I was babysitting Peeper's son, as usual. We were at my house while Peeper and the other 2 kids were at his house. I would help while his girlfriend worked. This particular day Peeper had free time, so he went up to Front Street; this is where all the fellas hung out. Across the street from the area they hung at on Front Street there's a store called, Star Market.

While the baby and I were chilling at my house; I received a phone call from my cousin Malinda. She said, "Peeper's been shot, they say it doesn't look good". That day...that call... changed my life. Soon after, there was another call. I don't remember who it was but someone on the other line said, "Bonnie get to the hospital, Peeper's dead!" I just started screaming and hollering. I remember grabbing his son tightly in my arms and rocking him and rocking him.

My son Meechy's girlfriend, Neeka rushed to my house to take the baby and I to the hospital. When I arrived at the hospital there were so many people already there. Family and friends alike were there crying and comforting each other. I looked over and I noticed there was some type of drama going on between Peeper's current girlfriend and his ex-girlfriend. There was chaos everywhere. It was like everything was going in slow motion; it was as if I was there, but I couldn't hear anything or anybody. I couldn't respond, all I heard was a bunch of jibber-jabber.

It seemed like everyone was trying to tell me something at once, but I couldn't comprehend anything they were trying to tell me. I just wanted to see my baby.

I could not cope with all the chaos so I started walking to find a different sitting area; the more private ones where they would place the family members. In one of the sitting areas, I went to; there sat Peeper's birth mom. I hadn't seen her in 30 years. She got up and hugged me; she reeked of booze. I just stared at her. I couldn't believe she was there.

The detective and doctors came out and asked which two family members were going to go back to identify him? There was no question in anyone's mind that I would be one of the people going back and nothing was going to stop me. His birth mom and I started walking down the hall. As we approached the room my legs started feeling weak. My baby was lying on a gurney with a white cover pulled up to his neck and a speck of blood on his nose. He looked like he was just sleeping peacefully. I attempted to touch him but was stopped by the officials. I started hollering, "PEEPER GET UP, PEEPER GET UP!", but there was no response. It hit me at this point that he was gone!

As his birth mom and I parted ways that day at the hospital; I knew I wasn't going to see her again not even at his funeral. I felt it in my spirit.

I tried to remain strong and make sense of what happened, but I just couldn't grasp everything at once. At this point my only concern was to not let his body sit in the morgue for much longer, so I started working on his funeral arrangements.

On April 1, 2017 I laid my son to rest. There were so many people, there wasn't an empty seat in the church. I had not noticed until the funeral was over and I turned so the casket could be carried out; then and only then did I realize how many people were lined up outside on the sidewalk. I was astonished by the crowd. I felt the love for my baby, he was loved by many.

After the funeral I started hearing different versions of that tragic day. None of the versions mattered to me because none of them were worth taking my son's life. I was told that 15-20 guys, including his killer Gerry Myles, were hanging out on Front St. across the street from Star Market, the neighborhood store. Peeper was seldom up there because he usually had to babysit the kids, but not this day.

A Caucasian female came up to score some dope, that's when Myles approached her telling her, "she better not buy anything from anyone before she pays him his $10 or else he was going to smack the shit out of her". They said that's when Peeper stepped up and said, "no you not, take that shit out in Bond Hill where you live". Peeper and Myles then started arguing Myles walked over to a car parked on the curve near the area they were standing and retrieved a gun. When he came back, he started shooting at the group of guys hitting Peeper and someone else. Everyone immediately started running.

Peeper was hit but he was still able to run. Myles chased him down like an animal and kept shooting him, hitting him seven times. The doctor's told me out of the seven shots fired six of them were not life-threatening. There was only one fatal shot.

Myles ran from the scene after killing Peeper. He was now a fugitive of the state and a coward. He remained hidden and unseen for some time. His face was plastered all over the news. They offered a reward for his capture and conviction.

I was sad and cried at times, but I hadn't genuinely grieved. I tried to keep busy by doing various things; I passed out thousands of flyers of the killer, Gerry Myles. I joined a group called "Who Killed My Son", I was trying to keep Peeper's death in the news I kept in contact with the Detectives Downtown and US Marshal's giving them any information I found. I had done all I could do on my end, but his killer was still running free. That's when full depression mode kicked in. I went into a very deep depression. Reality had sunken in. After Peeper's death, I kept his child for 3 weeks straight. It was like I was holding a part of him; I needed a part of him to feel better. I closed myself up in darkness, praying and crying. I knew I had to come up out of this slump I was in. I knew he wouldn't want me to just simply give up.

Lockland Police Detective called to inform me that no one was talking nor were they willing to write a statement. This devastated me. It was 15-20 of his so-called friends out there that night. One of them was supposed to be his cousin. This is a cousin who was at his house every day. After the cousin didn't talk, I guess the others felt why should they?

Now I felt devastated and betrayed! I was beginning to feel the tension brewing within the family. There were family members who started making up excuses as to why the cousin was not testifying. Most of the family members were upset and outraged, some stated, "it shouldn't even be a question." I could never see anyone of my family members hurt, harmed, or killed and not say anything. Without a shadow of a doubt I know I would have come forward.

I remember meeting a sergeant from The US Marshals and he promised me they would get the killer and gave me his personal cell number. We kept in contact on a regular basis. This man gave me life and hope.

On March 18th, 2018 that same sergeant from the US Marshals called me early that morning waking me up. He said, "Ms. Smith, I'm going to have Myles in my custody, but I need you to keep quiet about it and not leak a word until I call you back". It was so hard keeping the news from my family, but I had no choice. At this point, there were some family members I couldn't trust.

March 19, 2018 three days before Peeper's one-year balloon release. That morning the Sergeant called and asked me if I was sitting down. I let him know I was. He said, "We got him!" Tears of joy rolled out my eyes faster than water coming out of a faucet. I was screaming thank you, thank you, thank you Jesus! That's when I released the information to the family. Gerry Myles had fled to the state of Mississippi. He was found in a family member's trailer home in Yazoo City. Little did I know that this was just the beginning of more crying, more headaches, and more heartbreaks.

Soon after they apprehended Gerry Myles it was brought to my attention that just 12 days before killing my son, he had been released from state custody. He was on two-years probation for trafficking marijuana, cocaine and for having a 9 mm handgun. He was a dangerous man on the loose. If he had been kept in jail on those charges maybe my son would be alive today.

I remember being at one of the court hearings. The Prosecutor called me out into the hall to inform me they were dropping the murder charge because of a lack of witness cooperation and due to the poor quality of the surveillance video.

I completely lost it! I punched the wall and started crying & screaming. "Y'ALL JUST GOING TO LET THIS MAN KILL MY SON & GET AWAY WITH IT?" I yelled. I was furious and knew I had to do something. I told them I was going to call every news channel in the area and maybe they would be able to get answers from the judge. Maybe they would be able to get answers as to why Gerry Miles was released back into society while on probation and with felony charges.

Myles was no longer in jail for murder; his current charge is for violating his probation. His release date was quickly approaching. I continued to call the Prosecutor's office nonstop. I finally got the answers I had been praying for. Myles' murder charge had been reinstated before he was due to be released.

I was excited and I thought that maybe they got the Caucasian girl cleaned up. Maybe she was going to testify. Or maybe one of the guys decided to testify or even maybe the cousin who was up there finally wrote a statement and decided to testify. A lot of thoughts were running through my head. I was just so ecstatic that the killer would be getting charged with the death of my son.

On June 26, 2019 the Prosecutor called me and asked if I would agree to Gerry Myles pleading to eight years? They needed an answer by one that afternoon. My heart was broken but I knew I had to inform my family before making any decisions. I really wanted to take the case to trial but if we were to lose, they would never be able to charge him with this specific crime again. There is a law called "double jeopardy" which would prevent it.

The Prosecutors thought if I took it to trial; he could possibly walk out of jail the next day a free man. I had so much to think about. This was a big decision. I started a group chat on Facebook Messenger. I included Peeper's sister, kids, and other family members. I explained the situation and the important decision that had to be made. I had to tell them about all the roadblocks and issues I was facing. Everyone was just as shocked as I was but they each gave great feedback & supported me on my decision.

Although, eight years is hardly enough time for a murder crime; it's more like time for an armed robbery or something. Eight years is nothing in the grand scheme of things. However, I took the plea deal upon one stipulation of the plea. Gerry Miles would have to sit and allow myself or any one of my family members to speak to him. We needed to get something off our chest.

On July 16, 2019, my cousin Kisha, who is Peeper's older sister, my sister Temika, and I, as well as any other family member who wanted to, had a chance to address the man who killed my baby face to face. Right before sentencing, I was given the opportunity to say whatever I wanted to say to the man who took my son away from me and so many family members. I knew it wouldn't have changed the sentencing, but it did give me a sense of relief and it helped with my grieving process.

We can only pray for strength and comfort during our depression and grieving time. I know God got me through. Everyone grieves differently some longer than others. It's not a good feeling seeing someone that you raised in a casket before yourself. I never expected it. God said, "He would never leave me nor forsake me" and I trust Him. I know that Peeper's work here on earth was done and God needed him home in heaven.

Although Peeper's death was tragic, he continues to live on through the many lives that he touched. He was able to bless seven people with his organs; It touched my heart when I received a letter from the man who received his eyes.

He will also continue to live on through his children who will continue his legacy. He left behind 2 sons and 3 daughters, Derrick Jones, Ricky Lee Julious Jr, Rosemary Robinson, Seven Adams, and Aniya Julious.

I know Peeper is at peace now and this gives me solace.

Love you Peeper, Forever & Always...Until we meet again.

Mom

The Story of Tramon Matthews

My name is Shanell Nikki Thornton; family is everything to me. Being that I am an only child my mom and I are very close. Family is everything to me. When I found out I was pregnant for the second time, I was excited hoping it was my baby girl. I already had the pleasure of having my son, Jamon Matthews Jr. All I needed was a baby girl to complete my family. When the results came in, to my surprise I was not having the baby girl I had hoped for. The new addition to my family was a boy. Lord another boy was my thoughts when I heard the results but quickly after, I just hoped my baby boy was healthy. On April 1, 1999 my baby boy, Tra'Mon Matthews came into the world. He was beautiful, full of energy, he hardly ever cried, and he was healthy just as I asked, he never got sick as a child. We gave him the nickname Tray at a very young age, he loved to play, he was the jokester in the family. Tray was bad so we always joked about how bad he was and had the nerves to be scared to watch scary movies.

I felt like it was time to move away from Tallassee, the small city in Alabama I lived in. I decided a city call Montgomery in Alabama may be a nice change. I stayed the night at my cousin house so we could go out looking for the new place that I would call home. Tray and I Facetimed earlier that day around 10 am laughing about a situation between him and one of his female friends. We ended our phone call with him saying "I love you" as he did daily. It was a gloomy day and that night it was stormy, so I lay down to get some sleep. I received a call from my oldest son, Jamon who nickname is JJ. "Ma can you come to Tallassee Hospital" he said. "What's wrong" I asked. In a very calm voice, he told me that Tray been shot. I am about to throw on some clothes and I'm on my way I said. He was so calm that I did not think it was anything serious.

Being woke up out of my sleep, the call had caught me off guard but while I was getting dress, I continued to think about it, so I called JJ back. There was an important question that had not registered during the first short call due to sleep being over me. "JJ is he woke, I asked. "No" he responded, that's when the worry began to sat in. I called my mom to tell her what was going on. My cousin and I jump in the car and head to the hospital. My phone began to ding from my Facebook messenger. People had already started sending messages to my inbox saying, "sorry for your loss". It was making me upset; anxiety began to come over me and the tears started flowing. We had not even made it to the hospital, and here people go sending me these crazy messages. They don't even know what they're talking about, they have the wrong information, my baby was shot but he is not dead. What are they sorry for? Where do people get their nerves from to say such a thing? I was hoping it was just another rumor like many others that went around the small city when people heard things and put a story together from the very little details that they heard. I could feel myself filling with anger, the messages were upsetting me so much my cousin told me to put the phone down. My son JJ called a few times asking if I was on my way, I assured him that I was in route. We were driving as fast as we could in my cousin's older explorer. I called Jamon Sr., my children's father, to ask if he had made it to the hospital and if he had seen Tray. "Yes" he responded. "How was he doing" I asked, then the phone went silent. I was not sure if the phone hung up due to the reception because that would happen often in different areas in Alabama. As we continued our ride to the hospital It still did not register to me that I would not ever be taking my son home with me again.

When we arrived at the hospital, there were several people standing out front, we quickly jumped out the car. It was like I was in a daze, "where is Tray" I asked the first person I saw. There was no answer as if they did not hear what I said. I continued to walk towards the hospital, when I entered there was several others sitting inside. I asked the question again "where is Tray", my thoughts were for them to take me to the room they have him in, working on him to get him back to good health, but again I did not receive an answer. I looked over at my son JJ, "where is your brother" I asked. He put his head down and in a very low voice almost like a whisper he said, "mama he dead". I hit the ground and what happen immediately after that I don't know everything went blank.

When I woke up, I was in and area in the hospital I had never seen before after living in the area and visiting the hospital several times in the past. When I looked around the room, I saw my mother, some of my cousins, and other family members. I was still in a daze and was not sure of any of the details about how my son was killed. I remember hearing someone say they heard that someone rode by and shot him in a drive by shooting at the Capricorn Village Apartment in Tuskegee. I do not even remember what my response was to that or even if I responded at all. I recall my cousin Chinqua kept saying she was so sorry about Tray's death. I was not sure why her apologies stood out to me so much and why she kept saying it over and over again, but I later found out why. JJ, my oldest son and Rashad, my cousin Chinqua's son, was there at the time of the shooting. They were scared so they told the police the lie about the drive by shooting but later told the truth. Chinqua then told me that her son Rashad, Tray and JJ was sitting in the car, Rashad was playing with a gun, he put the gun against Tray arm and it accidently went off. Tray got out the car and began fanning his arm trying to cool his arm from the burning sensation. "Damn Tyrique you shot me" which was Rashad's nickname and those were the last words that came from his mouth before he collapsed, to never wake up again. I could hear the pity in Chinqua's voice. She was hurting; I could see it in her face. I was told she collapsed when she first heard what happen. I still love my cousin Chinqua she is one of the sweetest people I know. I could not blame her for what happen even though my feelings are so hurt.

We sat there for hours before I was able to go view Tray's body. The staff at the hospital was very polite. The nurse told me how hard they tried to resuscitate him. I felt like I was walking inside a nightmare. I felt like I needed someone to pinch me to wake me up, but I felt so numb I was not even sure I would feel it. When I walked into the room, he was laying there looking as if he was sleeping, there was not blood all over him like people think it be after someone is shot. When I touched him his body was cold, I held his hand, kissed and talked to him. The doctor looked at me and said, "if it eases the pain a little, I would like to let you know that he died quickly, he was already dead before he arrived at the hospital". It was time to leave out of the room with my baby boy, Tra'Mon Matthews, how do I walk out and leave him here? I want to take my baby with me, and it hurt me to my heart that he can't go. Before I walked out the door, I asked the doctor if he could please not bring my baby body out the hospital in a body bag.

When I stepped outside of the hospital it was full of people. I had not even notice, how many people was there when I arrived or recognized who was there. Everyone was outside talking, hugging and crying. There was so much love and support. Everything was still a daze for me, I felt like I was in a dream. I still felt like he was going to jump up and say April fools joking like he had joked so many times before. They brought him out the hospital on a gurney with a white sheet over him and put him into a white van. The parking lot of the hospital broke out into screaming and crying. All I could think about was getting to Cameron Faison, my youngest son that I had a year after Tra'Mon, he was taking it so hard. Even though I had not convinced myself that everything was going to be okay, I still had to make him feel that way as much as I could. I needed to be near him to hold and comfort him. The police had already taken my other son, JJ to the police station for questioning. I was glad he was not there to see his brother being brought out.

Rashad had already been taken to the police department as well. At this point I was not sure if he had been officially charged with the murder of my son or what they would be charging him with. A month after Tray's death I went to the jail with my cousin Chinqua to visit Rashad. When I looked at his face, he did not look the same and I could see sadness in his eyes. My family lost two of our boys, here he is 20 years old responsible for his cousin's death. A cousin that was so close to him they dressed alike and hung with one another often.

I get upset at him sometimes when I think back to what happened, but it is simply out of missing Tray. I know that it was an accident and Tyrek is suffering enough for it. I stopped going to the trials because it was too much for me. I do not want to see Rashad do jail time for killing Tray, it has taken a huge toll on him already. People feel like I am crazy for feeling this way, but he is my son, no one loves him more than me so if I found the strength to forgive Rashad, they need to accept how I feel. They are entitled to their feelings, but I would like them to keep their feelings away from me. Forgiveness is a part of healing and I am trying hard to get just a little piece of it.

Chinqua and I went out to eat after our visit to the jail. I told her how I wish Tray would have left me a baby. I wanted a piece of him here with me on earth while he spread his wings in heaven. When I got home that day, I logged into Facebook to occupy my mind. I had received an inbox from the Aunt of a young lady that Tray was involved with. I was in tears when I read the message, this time it was tears of joy. The message was to inform me that Tray had a daughter. I remembered seeing the young lady who had the baby at Tray's wake, and I asked her where her adorable baby girl was. I did not know the baby was still in the hospital, nor did I have any idea that she was Tray's daughter. I immediately told my family the news but did not get the response I thought I would. JJ and my mom wanted me to get a blood test to be sure she was ours, but Cameron and I had already accepted Zoey as ours. She was born April 2, 2017, a day after Tray's birthday. This was the blessing I needed to help me pull through my loss. When I looked at her face there was no need for a blood test, I knew she was his. Holding her, looking into her face was like holding Tray as a baby all over again. She was a spitting image of my Tray.

The Story of Adoniyah Pruitt

I was so excited to find out I was finally going to give birth to a boy. I was already a proud mother of four girls so the thought of having a boy put a smile on my face. As I laid there holding my only son, I decided to name him, Adoniyah Pruitt, which means my lord is Yahweh. He was given the nickname Poohda by the family shortly after he was born February 17, 1999. I never would have thought his life would have ended after only 18 years on earth. My name is Valerie Bell and I was fortunate enough to raise my children in a two-parent home. I felt that having two parents would be especially great for Poohda. There are some things that being a woman, I could not fully teach him when it comes to being, a man. Poohda was a great child, he was so loving, quiet, and on most occasions, I wish the girls would be more like him.

On November 17, 2017 I woke up to go to the restroom at 6 am. I always slept with the television on and just as I was getting out of bed the 6 o'clock news was coming on. I was sad to hear that a young man had been shot and killed on Behles Street which was only a street over from where I live in Lincoln Heights, a city inside of Cincinnati, Ohio. Shaking my head about all the senseless crime that happens in the neighborhood I will never forget the post I put on Facebook "Who got shot on Behles my condolences SMH". SMH is the acronym for shaking my head. The situation was very sad because everyone in the neighborhood knows one another or at least knows someone who would know the person or their family. It sucks the life out of me to find out that someone was my son.

Before I could lie back down there was loud banging on the door that sounded as if they were going to knock the door down. When my husband Charles opened the door, it was my daughter Lanita, who is my second to the youngest daughter. Before I could ask who got shot, she instantly began to ask Charles, "pops where Poohda". "Poohda, is in Avondale at Nisi's house" he responded. Nisi, is the nickname of my second to the oldest daughter. Poohda had been staying at her house to attend school online because I am not computer savvy so I would not be able to offer him any technical help if he needed it. I quickly intervened, telling them that Poohda did not go back to Nisi's he was still in Lincoln Heights from earlier. Lanita went on to say that someone called my nephew and told him they heard the young man that got shot was Lanita and Ketarah, which is my youngest daughter little brother. My mind felt as if I was going into shock as I felt like I knew right then and there it was my son. Then I felt a quick wave of confusion. The news reported that the incident occurred between 2 am and 2:30 am, it is now 6:15 am so the family should have already been told if it was their love one especially since everyone knows of each other in the neighborhood. Despite the confusion in my heart I knew it was my son and the tears began to fall.

We decided to drive around the corner to see if anyone was still out so we could see what was going on. When I saw all the Detectives and the Sheriff from the Lincoln Heights Police Department still standing at the scene, I began to cry uncontrollably. "Is that my son" I asked the sheriff, barely being able to get the words out. The sheriff told me to hold on for a moment let him speak to one of the detectives. By the time the detective came over and asked me to sit in his car I was hysterical, so much so I did not even notice another detective was sitting in the back of the car. He began to ask me what felt like a thousand questions. My mind was all over the place however, I remember the most important ones. He told me to describe my son, I went on to tell him he was 5 feet 5 inches tall, had dreads, and he was real stocky built. He asked if I knew of anyone my son had been into it with, I told him no, that my son did not bother anyone. I then remembered around August he had gotten into it with a boy named Eddie at a party he had gone to in a section of Lincoln Heights that everyone referred to as up on the hill. The area is no more than ten minutes walking from my house and three minutes in a car. One of Eddie's friends pulled out a gun on Poohda during the altercation, but I did not know his name. Eddie always hung with a group of guys and they constantly picked with Poohda when they would see him out or at school. Poodha pretty much kept to himself and would often be alone. Eddie would see him walking around alone and he did not know who he was, so he felt like that was grounds enough to pick with him. Poohda was upset and had expressed that Eddie was only messing with him because he was with a crowd of boys. Two days after school started Poohda saw Eddie in the hallway at school standing at his locker and none of his friends were around. Poohda approached Eddie, they fought and Poohda was expelled from school. The incident is why he was attending school online and had to live with my daughter. Avondale was only about fifteen minutes from where I live, it is a rough area and I knew that he did not know a lot of people there. I was worried about him staying out there and constantly told my daughter to keep an eye on him so for him to be killed right next to home was devastating.

I was sitting in the car with the window cracked because my nerves were bad, I needed a cigarette. It was very hard to sit there while waiting for them to confirm if the young man, who had been rushed away in an ambulance hours ago and died on the way to the hospital before we even knew anything was going on was my one and only son. My husband Charles and one of the detectives stood on the sidewalk near the car talking. "Is it him" Charles asked. My face was already full of tears before he could answer yes. I already felt in my soul that God had gained another angel along with my mother and brother. Thoughts started to run through my head about my last conversation with my son, Adoniyah. My friend Andi and I picked him up from my daughter's house because he wanted to spend the night at his sister, Lanita's house. We arrived back at my house and I told him to clean up his bedroom. When he came back downstairs, I asked him if he had any money and he said no, so I gave him $20. He asked for a jacket to put on and I could not find one, so I gave him a sweater to put on. Even the smallest memories mean so much when you lose a loved one. When he was leaving out the door with his friend Neimiah and his mom who came over to pick him up I said, "I love you", he told me he loved me back then left. I never thought that would be the last time I would have seen my son alive. I called him shortly after he left because Charles noticed that even though he cleaned his bedroom, his bathroom was not clean. I spoke to him about it over the telephone, when he still had not made it back to clean the bathroom, I texted him. That was the last conversation I had with my child.

Everyone was trying to find out what happened to Adoniyah, there was a lot of gossip, but no one was sure. One thing for certain and two things for sure is that Jason Rutherford also known as Tuna had something to do with the death of my son. Tuna and Poohda were like family, they share the same cousin. The area my son was killed in was right in front of his grandmother's house. The detective came to my house between 12 am and 12:30 am that afternoon. He told us they came to my house that night shortly after the incident happened, but no one answered the door. We explain to them we were sleep and did not hear them at the door. He then began to tell us what happen to my son. I tried to collect my thoughts, but my mind was just not there. So many thoughts were going through my mind, my baby is gone, and I could not protect him. I was wishing that it could have been me instead.

The detective began to tell us that they questioned Jason. He is the one who called 911 and was on the scene holding Poohda when the police arrived. He told them three guys dressed in all black tried to rob him and Poohda was shot. The officer explained that Jason tried to ride in the ambulance with Poohda, but they needed to speak to him at the time because he was the only witness. Jason did not become a suspect until the K9 kept leading them back to his car. As they asked more questions the story was beginning to get more confusing. Then the gossip began going around the neighborhood. People began to say that it happened, because Poohda set it up for Tuna to get robbed. Jason did not breakdown and tell the truth until after we told him that Adoniyah did not make it said the detective. Jason then admitted that he was the shooter, he said he had been drinking Lean and taken Percocet and had fallen to sleep in the car with his gun on his lap. He said when Poohda walked up to the car it scared him, he grabbed the gun and shot. When he noticed that is was Poohda he ran in the house to hide the gun. He ran back outside to hold him while he called 911 and continue to hold him until the ambulance arrived. Adoniyah was shot in the chest with a 45 hollow point bullet. He fought as long as he could but had internal bleeding and died on the way to the hospital in the ambulance.

I was grateful to hear that Tuna did not run off and leave my son lying on the ground to die alone. May 3, 2018 was the first day that I would see Jason again after he murdered my son. He had been held in the Hamilton County Justice Center since Adoniyah murder in November on a one million dollars bond. Jason was facing 25 years for the murder of my son. I wanted him to pay for the mistake he made that cost my son his life. If he hadn't chosen made the chose to sell or use drugs my son would still be here today. As I stood in front of the court to speak my lip was trembling and I held up the best I could. It was a hard decision to make but I decided to show some compassion for Jason. My daughters did not share my compassion and they wanted him to be sentenced to death. They could not understand how I could feel any empathy for him at all, but I am spiritually in a different place then they are in life, so I know why they do not understand. The sound of Tuna's voice on the 911 call had touched my heart. He did not hang up the phone even after the police arrived and I could hear the pain in his voice as they questioned him when they arrived. My decision resulted in the judge reducing the twenty- five years sentence to a ten years sentence. I told him that I forgive him for the mistake he made that November night. The angry side of me still wanted him to have some sleepless nights thinking about my son as he was passing away slowly in that driveway. My daughters and I had different emotions towards him. It upset my daughter Lanita that Jason was asked if he had anything he wanted to say, and he said no. She told him that she would never forgive him because he did not even have the decency to apologize for what he had done so he deserved everything that he was going to get.

I will never forget what happened to my son that night, but I am at peace with it. I believe that the trial being over and knowing that justice is being served for Poohda has helped to bring me some closure. All I can do is take things one day at a time. Some days are good, and some are bad but every day I say" long live Poohda".

Lightning Source UK Ltd.
Milton Keynes UK
UKHW021451070620
364500UK00002B/324